"David Arraya's *Conscious Hospitality* is a powerful reminder that the future of our industry depends not only on service excellence, but on conscious leadership. With clarity and authenticity, David offers a framework that elevates human connection to its rightful place at the heart of hospitality. This is essential reading for any leader committed to shaping the next era of our craft."

—Simon Casson • CEO, Corinthia Hotels

"Throughout my career, I've learned that the greatest teams are built on trust, discipline, and shared purpose. What David Arraya shares in *Conscious Hospitality* goes far beyond the hospitality industry—it's a philosophy of leadership that speaks to the human side of excellence. His words remind us that true greatness is not just measured in results, but in how we show up for, and with, others. This book is a powerful guide for anyone who wants to lead with heart, clarity, and impact."

—Raphaël Varane • World Cup champion and former professional footballer

"At Six Senses, we believed that hospitality is a pathway to human connection, wellbeing, and transformation. In *Conscious Hospitality*, David brings this truth to life with wisdom, humility, and heart. His framework is not just a leadership model—it's a blueprint for living and leading with intention. This book will inspire anyone who believes in the power of elevated, human-centered service."

—Neil Jacobs • founder, Wild Origins; former CEO, Six Senses

"Since I first met David at a three-hour dinner in Austin years ago, I've noticed there's something special about this dude. He's kind, curious, thoughtful, and a servant leader. In a world obsessed with productivity, David reminds us that presence is the ultimate performance enhancer. This book will change how you lead, parent, and exist in the world."

—Ryan Hawk • host, *The Learning Leader Show*; author, *Welcome to Management*, *The Pursuit of Excellence*, and *The Score That Matters*

"*Conscious Hospitality* is a reckoning. A quiet one. David Arraya reminds us that hospitality is not built with checklists, but with attention. That leadership is not performance, but presence. This book speaks to those who understand that the most powerful thing we bring into a room is ourselves, and that the rarest luxury left is being fully here."

—Bashar Wali • founder and chief executive, ThisAssembly

"Life is a remarkable gift that invites us to grow and evolve. David entered my life at a decisive moment in my career and personal journey, and reminded me of the importance of self care and reconnecting with oneself to stay true to purpose. This mindset is at the heart of how we develop future leaders and today's emerging leaders are fortunate to have voices like David's guiding them. This book is timely and necessary. *Conscious Hospitality* reflects what our industry should stand for because hospitality is, above all, about people, presence, and genuine connection."

—Mano Soler • managing director, Les Roches Marbella

"*Conscious Hospitality* is an invitation to grow wiser, not just more successful. David Arraya blends the craft of hospitality with the inner work of leadership, offering a thoughtful guide for leaders ready to integrate experience, purpose, and presence. This is leadership through the lens of a modern elder—deeply human, grounded, and meaningful."

—Chip Conley • founder, Modern Elder Academy; bestselling author, *Wisdom at Work*

Conscious Hospitality

Lessons in Leadership, Humanity, and Purpose From a Life in Luxury Hospitality

David Arraya

Global Hospitality Futurist

Published by Maison Vero
3002 Dow Avenue, Suite 112
Tustin, CA 92780

Inquiries may be directed to: Maison Vero, 3002 Dow Avenue, Suite 112 Tustin, CA 92780, or info@graymilleragency.com.

For information about special discounts for bulk purchases, please call (949)333-4872 or email info@graymilleragency.com.

Maison Vero is a partner brand of The Gray + Miller Agency, a speaking, literary, and talent consortium.

For more information on the talent represented by The Gray + Miller Agency, or to bring any of our thought leaders to your organization or live event, please visit our website at graymilleragency.com

Cover Design: Zach Sharples

Manufactured in the United States of America

Paperback: 978-1-969508-24-0   E-book: 978-1-969508-25-7
Hardcover: 978-1-969508-23-3

TABLE OF CONTENTS

Foreword

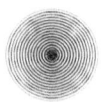

I've spent years watching hospitality chase the wrong things.

Thread counts. Magazine "best-of" lists. AI personalization engines. Loyalty programs. The industry builds increasingly elaborate experiences while sometimes forgetting that the best moments are much more subtle and predicated on detail, empathy, and understanding.

David Arraya understands this. I've followed his career through some of the most sophisticated and interesting properties in the world, but reading *Conscious Hospitality* revealed something beyond professional success. This is the story of a hotelier who discovered that everything he'd been taught about leadership was built on a foundation that couldn't hold.

Early in the book, David describes standing in his son's playroom, phone in hand, while the boy desperately tries to get his attention. When he finally snaps at his son, his wife delivers a line that belongs on every leader's desk: "You're here, but you're not really here."

That sentence contains the entire thesis of this book. It also contains the central crisis of modern leadership.

We've created an always-on work culture that rewards distracted availability but misses the importance of actual presence. We've SOP'd hospitality to the point where we've forgotten it's fundamentally about human connection. We measure everything except what matters most: the quality of focus and attention we bring into a room.

What strikes me about David's approach is that he refuses to separate professional leadership from personal life. He writes about managing a crisis at Six Senses Ibiza and putting his children to bed using the same vocabulary—presence, attunement, nervous system regulation. This isn't category confusion. The skills that make you an exceptional hotelier (reading a room, sensing what's unsaid, creating safety) are the same skills that make you a conscious parent and partner.

The framework he offers sounds deceptively simple: presence, authenticity, intention, empathy, integration. But try living it. Most of us operate from patterns we never consciously chose. We're reactive when we mean to be responsive. We perform when we want to be present. We manage behavior when we should be attending to energy.

Here's David's insight: hospitality at its highest level isn't about what you do—it's about what you transmit. And that transmission is determined by your internal state.

When you walk into a meeting anxious and scattered, your team feels it before you speak. When you greet a guest while mentally drafting an email, they register your absence even if they can't name it. We're constantly broadcasting and receiving emotional signals. You can engineer the perfect welcome sequence, but if the person delivering it is disconnected, the guest will feel the dissonance.

This is what separates this book from typical leadership literature. David isn't offering tips for better outcomes. He's describing a fundamental reorientation—from managing behavior to influencing energy, from directing action to creating conditions, from force to resonance.

There's a moment in the book where David finds a housekeeper crying in a back corridor. She'd made a relatively small mistake and angered her line manager. David doesn't fix her problem or deliver a pep talk. He sits with her, tells her about his own failures, and asks what she needs. The conversation takes maybe ten minutes. That housekeeper became one of the resort's best team members—not because David solved anything, but because he changed how she felt about herself and her work at that moment.

That's the thing this book unlocks: learning to be the kind of presence that allows others to rise. To regulate yourself so completely that your calm becomes available to others. To lead from alignment rather than ambition.

The hospitality industry loves to talk about innovation. But we rarely acknowledge that the most important variable in amazing guest experiences is the leader's internal state. David's central argument—that we must attend to nervous systems, not just performance metrics—is the most practical, difficult work there is.

This approach requires difficult self-reflection. It requires confronting your own patterns, your inherited ways of leading, the parts of yourself you'd rather not examine. It asks you to slow down in an industry built on speed and demands presence in a productivity culture.

Near the end of the book, David shares something his daughter said to him: "I like when you're not in a hurry." David's core point here, and something I've noticed register strongly with discerning guests, is that true luxury is unhurried presence: the gift of complete attention.

If you work in hospitality, this book belongs on your desk—not to replace your service standards but to remind you why they exist. But importantly, the lessons transcend hotels. If you lead people in any capacity, this is an invitation to ask a different question. Not "How do I get better results?" but "How do I become the kind of person who creates conditions for excellence?"

Service, at its deepest level, is about seeing people. This book is about learning to do that—first with yourself, then with everyone you lead.

—Colin Nagy

Global brand strategy and marketing at Meta, columnist

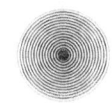

INTRODUCTION
My Journey Into Hospitality

"Hospitality is not to change people,
but to offer them a space where change can take place."

—Henri Nouwen

I've known I wanted to be in hospitality since I was eighteen years old. I had just returned to my native Bolivia after a year in the south of France, ready to conquer the world—one hotel at a time. I loved my time in France, where I discovered I could add value to a team in much the same way soccer had allowed me to do throughout my childhood. Once I left, everything changed. I could reinvent myself—become whatever I wanted to be. A blank slate. What I didn't realize, however, was that this reinvention would take me on a twenty two-year global adventure. More importantly, I would exchange my first passion for another.

A few years earlier, I was sitting with my wise grandmother, Bebita, telling her about my dreams and ambitions. Bebita came from a wealthy and respected family in Bolivia, and her expectations of others were incredibly high. In her home, we always had to be well dressed and well behaved. The house felt like a museum, filled with relics she collected during her travels around the world. On Wednesday nights she would take my younger brother and me to the Radisson Hotel in La Paz for crepes.

"I'm going to be a soccer star, Bebita! I'm going to live all over the world and play for the best clubs of all!"

She would quickly counter, "No, no, David; you will be an ambassador—or a hotelier."

I'd smile, ignore her words, and head back to the crepe line for another serving.

Looking back, life's paths aren't as unexpected as they seem in the moment. I once heard that a true genius is the one who can connect the dots forward, and I now understand the power of those words.

Bolivia is a country of deep-rooted indigenous traditions and vibrant culture, yet also of clear social divides. As the last country colonized in the Americas, it became a meeting point for indigenous tribes fleeing European conquistadores. Bolivia is home to the largest number of South American indigenous communities, and thus recognizes many official languages. After I left Bolivia in 2003, the country entered a revolution that led to a coup d'état and began what many experienced as a thirteen-year dictatorship under Evo Morales.

At the time of my upbringing, a small percentage of the population held a large majority of the country's wealth. The High Society—*La High*—was a tight group of mostly Spanish-descendant families who interacted with one another in nearly every aspect of life. I belonged to *La High* through my mother's side, which enjoyed significant privilege and respect. My father's side, however, did not. My grandfather was a professional soccer player which, in the Bolivia of the 1940s, meant you were making small ends meet.

My father, who lived a very humble life prior to meeting my mother, constantly reminded us of our deep Bolivian roots, the importance of humility, and the dark sides of privilege. He taught us to treat every individual with respect, never judge by appearances, and continually appreciate the opportunities we had—for they should never be taken for granted. As a result, my upbringing carried a nuanced, paradoxical mix of privilege and groundedness.

One of the privileges I enjoyed was attending the American Cooperative School, a private school for affluent Bolivian families and the children of embassy functionaries. I grew up in embassy homes, speaking different languages, and sampling different cultures through my friends. On weekends, I'd eat ceviche with my Peruvian friends or Domino's pizza with my American companions. Early on, this international community introduced me to diverse perspectives and values, offering a blend of Bolivian roots and a global outlook that would shape me in ways I couldn't have predicted.

Most of us shared a dream back then—the idea of building a life and career in the United States, the "land of opportunity," where ambition and hard work promised meaning and purpose. My four older brothers had already "made it" in the U.S.; I wanted that too.

Even though I formed part of this privileged slice of society, I remained deeply connected to my Bolivian roots through my family and, especially, through soccer. My grandfather was the first Bolivian goalkeeper to make it internationally and went on to coach the national team. I wanted to follow in his footsteps—not just on the field, but in life. To him, soccer was a way to understand life—a training ground for discipline, teamwork, and resilience. Of all my brothers, I was the one who shared not only his passion but, to some extent, his talent. I carried those values with me on and off the field, learning that the sum of our efforts together is always greater than any individual achievement.

I played soccer throughout my entire upbringing and, when I wasn't playing, I was dreaming of becoming a star. Back then, I wasn't thinking about luxury hotels or Michelin-starred restaurants. My journey into hospitality didn't start in a grand lobby; it started with a soccer ball.

I was the kid organizing matches in the schoolyard, joining leagues on weekends, staying after practice to perfect my passes, and studying my coaches as closely as I studied the game. From an early age, I was drawn to the dynamics of teamwork, the power of discipline, and the subtle but essential art of leadership.

I knew every player and devoured my weekly copy of *El Gráfico*, with recaps of the best leagues around the world. I wouldn't miss a televised match and became a die-hard Manchester United fan.

Academics weren't my priority in high school. My focus was narrow: sports, girls, and friends—in that order. On the field, I often became captain of whatever team I joined. I was fascinated by what made a group click, how culture shaped performance, and why some teams just worked. I watched the Chicago Bulls, San Antonio Spurs, and Los Angeles Lakers win championship after championship and saw my beloved Manchester United dominate European soccer under Sir Alex Ferguson. If I wasn't glued to the TV, I had a ball at my feet or in my hands.

When high school ended, reality hit—a pivot point. Many of my peers headed to the U.S. for college, but my family couldn't afford to send me. As the fifth of six boys, you can imagine how quickly money ran dry. I was gutted. I tried to earn a soccer scholarship, but my grades weren't strong enough. I was angry at myself for not putting more effort into my studies. My mother was heartbroken that she couldn't open that door for me, and she went looking for alternatives that might still help me pursue my dream.

That disappointment led to a different opportunity: a cultural exchange program in the south of France.

I joined a cohort of forty young adults from around the world who would spend a year abroad together. In exchange, my parents hosted another young adult in our home. The application asked for my top three priorities for the year. I wrote: "Live by the ocean; speak a new language; work with people."

I landed a placement at *Centre Familial Le Lazaret*, a humble, government-subsidized holiday resort in Sète, France. It was nothing like the polished hotels I'd later work in, but it was real. I started at the bar and quickly rotated through the entire operation—housekeeping, restaurant, front desk, guest experience (recreation), and engineering—until I eventually took on a leadership role as recreation manager.

One week I was behind the bar; the next I was folding sheets or painting an entire building. The environment was full of people, movement, and purpose. I was hooked.

Just like in soccer, I thrived when surrounded by a team—when every day felt like game day and every interaction held the possibility of making someone feel seen and cared for. I started noticing how music affected the bar's mood, how the timing of a smile could brighten someone's night, and how surprising a table of thirteen German women with a round of beers could turn into one heck of an evening—but that's a story for another time.

What I realized was that I *loved* making people feel good—not just through service, but through connection. Most importantly, it reinforced that coaching and leadership mattered.

I knew this was my path.

The year flew by, and by the end I couldn't wait to explore hospitality—what I knew then as "recreation"—and make it my lifelong career. I began to see hospitality as something more than a job. It wasn't just about managing accommodations or delivering services; it was about human connection.

A single smile, a thoughtful gesture, a kind word—these could transform someone's experience. Hospitality had the potential to make people feel seen, valued, and cared for. That struck me deeply. Here was a field where I could bring together my love of teamwork, my drive for excellence, and my desire to make a meaningful impact on people's lives.

That experience lit a fire in me: I wanted to become a hotelier. Not just any hotelier—I wanted to lead world-class hotels around the globe and create magical experiences that left people better than when they arrived. If I was going to abandon my dream of playing for the top soccer teams, then I would join—and help lead—the best hotel teams in the world.

Over the last twenty two years, I've done just that—living, working, and leading across thirteen locations: New York, Miami, Hong Kong, Hawaii, Austin, Aspen, Riviera Maya, Ibiza, Madrid, and Alicante. I've had the privilege of working for top luxury hotel brands and learning from a remarkable group of world-class hoteliers whom I now call friends.

Each stop taught me something meaningful:

The Pierre, New York—I discovered what five-star excellence really means. Every detail matters. The polish, the standards, the heritage—it's hospitality at its most refined. I learned to deliver with poise, and I learned how easy it can be to lose yourself in the performance of it all.

Fontainebleau Miami Beach—I saw what it takes to operate a massive, high-volume property—one with an independent owner and brand that brought together professionals from many organizations for a single challenge. Fundamentals became non-negotiable: clarity, communication, and consistency were the glue that held everything together.

Swire Hotels (Miami and Hong Kong)—My first taste of lifestyle hospitality: elevated, bold, a little rebellious. I learned to lead with creativity and to see how long-term vision shapes culture. It was also my first experience inside a company with more than a century of legacy. Reputation, patience, and respect for the long game became real.

Four Seasons Lānai, Hawaii—One of the most pivotal experiences of my career. A small island, a tight-knit team, and a cultural expectation to understand and embrace the "Aloha Spirit"—layered over Lānai's history as a pineapple plantation for more than fifty years. Here, I learned humility: to listen, to slow down, and to respect a way of being that was both ancient and alive.

Four Seasons Austin—I joined a leadership team that was proud, spirited, and forward-thinking—a well-oiled machine optimizing every day. I learned the power of a global company, and how high-performing professionals want autonomy and empowerment. This was a time of major growth—personally and professionally—as I learned to lead through creativity, crisis, and change. It was also the beginning of my awakening, which we'll explore later.

Hotel Jerome, Auberge Collection, Aspen—The world was upside down. COVID had thrown a wrench into everything we thought we knew. I had to show up with empathy and resilience while guiding the team and keeping morale strong. We returned to the basics of hospitality, severely understaffed, everyone jumping in. It was a period of profound connection across our industry amid upheaval and the decimation of job opportunities.

Etéreo, Auberge Collection, Riviera Maya—A new build. A fresh concept. A blank slate. A new cycle. This project was about culture—intentional, lived, and shared. Not just a brand guide or a mission statement, but a living, breathing set of values practiced daily. We were on a mission to bring Mexico to life through this property, and everything we did reflected that. The lessons were about family, trust, and believing in something bigger than yourself.

Six Senses Ibiza and Nômade People—Hospitality took on a new dimension. These weren't just places to stay—they were places where people came to grow, heal, and connect. Something shifted in me. I started to realize that when this work is done with heart and presence, it isn't "just hospitality."

It's something deeper.
It's Conscious Hospitality.

Living all over the world has given me the opportunity to engage with far more people than most. In writing this book—and running the numbers—I realized I have led over 16,500 team members and 850 leaders across cultures, countries, and continents. I've had thousands upon thousands of conversations about guest issues, challenges to resolve, and creative solutions in environments that demanded excellence. I dealt with people, through people, for people.

Why am I telling you this? To stroke my ego?

A former version of me might have said, "Maybe."

The new me shares this to invite you into a new way of thinking.

The truth is, this crazy adventure I call hospitality became more than a career; it became a way of life. As you can imagine, that's true not only for me but for my brave and patient family as well. I took my role as a hotelier seriously, and my family assimilated into the cultures we entered because they took their roles seriously too.

These experiences shaped my leadership style, turning the whole journey into a very human experiment. Through countless interactions—solving problems, having honest conversations, and listening closely to team members across the industry—I developed a unique understanding of people. I came to see how differently individuals think, communicate, and respond. One-size-fits-all approaches rarely work; adaptability is essential. And yet, at our very core, we share several important attributes in common.

This book is the result of those experiences, lessons, conversations, insights, and realizations. It's for the leader who wants to go deeper, for the parent who wants to be more present, and for the entrepreneur who's chasing purpose—not just profit.

Because hospitality is not just an industry. It's a way of being.

> Hospitality is not just an industry.
> It's a way of being.

And now, I invite you to explore what that means—for your life, your leadership, and your legacy.

This book guides you through the philosophy and practice of Conscious Hospitality—a way of leading, living, and connecting rooted in presence, authenticity, intention, empathy, and integration. Whether you're a hospitality professional, an entrepreneur, a team leader, a parent, or simply someone seeking a deeper way to engage with life, I've written it to be both inspiring and practical.

I've divided the book into three parts: Embracing a Hospitality Mindset, The Conscious Hospitality Framework, and Applying Conscious Hospitality. Each chapter builds on the last, starting with foundational concepts and moving into applied wisdom across work, home, and self.

Along the way, you'll find:

- Personal stories from my twenty two-year journey in luxury hospitality, leadership, and fatherhood—real moments of challenge, growth, and awakening.
- Timeless principles drawn from ancient wisdom, modern science, and leadership psychology.
- Tangible practices and tools—from rituals to reflection prompts, journaling exercises to team practices—you can apply immediately in your daily life and leadership.
- Quotes and insights to anchor each idea with clarity and depth.
- Narrative storytelling that keeps you engaged, weaving philosophy with human experience.

This book is not meant to be rushed through. Move at your own pace. Pause when something resonates. Re-read when something challenges you. Use it as a mirror, a map, and a companion.

At the end of this book, you will find a complete version of my Conscious Living Library—a curated collection of the books, podcasts, conversations, and teachings that have influenced my journey. Think of it as an open invitation to continue exploring. Use it as inspiration, as a companion, and as a continuation of the expansion of consciousness that this book invites.

Because this journey—*your* journey—is yours to continue.

Mastery isn't a destination; it's a lifelong dialogue with curiosity.

Read it cover to cover or return to the chapters that speak to your current moment. Whether you're looking to improve team culture, reconnect with your purpose, or create deeper connections at home, this book will meet you there.

Above all, this is not a book to admire from a distance—it's a book to live.

Because the more consciously we live, the more consciously we lead. And the more consciously we lead, the more consciously we love.

So take a breath.
Settle in.
And allow these pages to meet you exactly where you are.

Let's begin the journey together.

PART I

EMBRACING A HOSPITALITY MINDSET

CHAPTER 1

The Mirrors of Awakening

"You don't find the meaning of life; you create it by finding yourself."

—Naval Ravikant

Every awakening begins with a mirror.
In my case, there were two.

The first wake-up call came during the Four Seasons General Manager Academy—a highly selective leadership program where top performers from across the company gathered to elevate their skillset and prepare for senior leadership. I was proud to be there. At the time, it felt like a badge of honor, a recognition of how far I had come. I walked in confident—maybe a little too confident—expecting to be validated, seen, celebrated.

Instead, I got a reflection.

On the very first day, we went through a process of 360-degree feedback, which included anonymous input from my colleagues, direct reports, mentors, and family. I had requested feedback from people I trusted, people whose opinions I valued. I expected validation, a reassurance that my trajectory was solid.

What I wasn't prepared for was the pattern that emerged.
One comment in particular stopped me in my tracks:

"David is great at getting people to the dock, but he leaves without checking if everyone got on the boat."

It landed quietly, gently, but it cut deeper than I expected. There was no cruelty, only truth. And it pierced because deep down, I had already sensed it.

I was leading with vision and urgency but missing something critical: presence. In my pursuit of results, I had become disconnected from my people. I was

15

moving too fast, assuming they were with me—when in fact, they were often left scrambling.

This wasn't just about leadership style. It was about how I showed up—or didn't—for those around me. I started to question everything: my habits, my energy, and the quality of my relationships. I left the GM Academy with more questions than answers.

Then came the second mirror, two weeks later, sharper and closer to home.

It was a Saturday. I was standing in the playroom while my kids played, my phone in hand, reading emails. My son, Cruz, was trying to get my attention, but I was lost in the scroll. Frustrated after several ignored attempts, he reached up and knocked the phone out of my hand. It clattered on the tile—louder than necessary—but it was what followed that truly changed me forever.

I snapped. I picked him up and shook him out of frustration. Cruz's eyes were not angry, not scared—they were hurt. Jessica, my wife, intervened immediately. She took him from my arms and looked at me with frustration and desperation.

"David, something has to change," she said. "You're here, but you're not really here."

Her words echoed the feedback I had received just weeks earlier. And just like that, the mirrors were clear. I had become a stranger to presence—not only at work but at home.

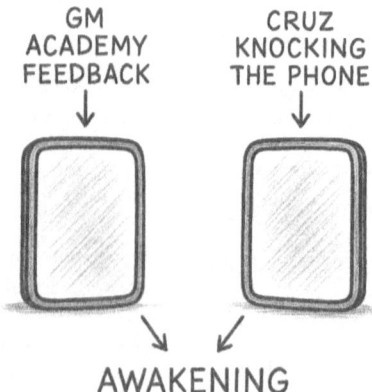

My phone was the first thing I touched in the morning and the last thing I saw at night. I answered emails at dinner. I scrolled LinkedIn while my kids talked about their day. I walked through meetings with one eye on my notifications and another on the clock. I wasn't leading with clarity—I was reacting with speed.

Always slightly ahead, never fully here.

The truth is, I had trained myself to be externally responsive at the cost of internal awareness. My identity had become wrapped in urgency. I confused movement with momentum. I thought being always available meant I was always leading.

Something HAD to change.

Immediately following the traumatic event at home, I contacted the coach who had facilitated the 360-degree review at the Academy. "I need help!" I said to her, and we agreed to jump on a call.

That one-hour session changed my life. I began the work, peeling back the layers. What I uncovered was something many of us live with: a default, ego-led programming based on urgency, perfectionism, and external validation.

I realized I was living out patterns I didn't consciously choose. I had been conditioned to equate leadership with control, parenting with discipline, and success with speed. But these were inherited scripts—not conscious values. I was running old software on outdated hardware.

But presence isn't about proximity. It's about energy. And I was giving mine away, little by little, without even realizing it.

This shift led me to understand the power of awareness and that it is only in stillness that we notice, and that in noticing, we serve. But noticing is not the end of the journey—it is just the beginning. What I had stumbled upon in those moments of raw feedback and painful honesty was not just a correction to my habits, but a realization of a deeper truth: leadership is not about how fast we move, but about how present we are while moving.

This realization became an invitation to slow down, to peel back inherited patterns, and to begin leading from a place that was less about proving and more about being.

That invitation became the first step on a lifelong path—the path of Conscious Hospitality.

CHAPTER 2

Awareness Through Distraction

"Between stimulus and response, there is a space.
In that space is our power to choose our response.
In our response lies our growth and our freedom."

—Viktor Frankl

Awareness rarely arrives as a celebration. More often, it arrives as a confrontation—a moment when reality refuses to bend to our momentum, and we are left face-to-face with ourselves. For me, that moment came during one of the most pivotal conversations of my life. My coach listened as I described the friction I felt—at home, at work, in my own mind. Something wasn't right. Something in me had drifted far from the man, father, and leader I believed myself to be.

She let the words settle, then asked a question with a softness so disarming that it cut straight through all my practiced explanations:

"David... when was the last time you were fully present?"

I opened my mouth, but no answer came—not because I didn't want to answer, but because I truly didn't know. I could recount where I had been, what I had done, and who I had spoken to. But I couldn't remember the last moment I had actually *inhabited*. I had been everywhere, but nowhere fully. Moving constantly, producing endlessly, performing competence while slowly distancing myself from my own life.

She continued, with a clarity that struck like lightning cutting through fog:

"What you're experiencing isn't a failure of leadership or parenting. It's a symptom of distraction. And distraction is not the enemy. Unawareness is."

It was the first time I realized that my challenge wasn't rooted in external demands. I wasn't losing myself to my phone—I was losing myself to my mind. I wasn't overwhelmed because life was chaotic—I was overwhelmed because I was unconscious within it. I had become so accustomed to operating at speed that I had forgotten how to *feel* my life as it was unfolding.

The assignment she gave me afterwards was startling in its simplicity: *notice*.

Notice when I reached for my phone.
Notice when my breath shortened.
Notice when my mind drifted ahead of the moment.
Notice the times I wasn't really listening, only reacting.
Notice the ways I rushed through even the most intimate spaces of my life.

It sounded easy. It wasn't.

Noticing meant confronting the truth of how often I lived on autopilot. It meant seeing the patterns I had normalized: scanning emails before saying good morning to my wife; rehearsing the next meeting while walking into the current one; drifting mentally when my children spoke; occupying rooms physically while my mind lingered elsewhere; scrolling mindlessly on social media. I was all over the place, and yet nowhere at the same time. Every moment of my day, I was thinking of what came next. I rushed into my meetings, without preparation. I reacted emotionally to any situation. I was constantly on edge.

Awakening does not arrive gently. It arrives with the discomfort of seeing the gap between who you think you are and how you are actually living.

As I began to notice, I saw the deeper architecture of modern life. We live in a system that rewards immediacy over depth, velocity over clarity, reactivity over reflection. Notifications ping, calendars overflow, information pulses through every spare moment, and we internalize the belief that responsiveness equals commitment. In that environment, presence becomes rare—not because we lack the capacity for it, but because we have stopped cultivating it.

For years, I believed that my speed was a strength. I moved quickly. I solved problems before they escalated. I anticipated needs instinctively. Those abilities made me effective in hospitality, where momentum is part of the culture. But I had mistaken activity for awareness. I had confused motion with meaning. I had adopted a rhythm that moved me forward professionally while quietly pulling me away from myself.

That realization did not break me. It woke me up.

NARROW FOCUS
Limited Awareness

WIDE FOCUS
Expanded Awareness
& Presence

As I observed my days with greater honesty, I recognized how my attention shaped not only my experience, but also the atmosphere around me. When my mind was scattered, I carried that fragmentation into meetings, conversations, and even family moments. When I was rushed, others felt the acceleration. When I was distracted, it didn't matter how much I cared—my presence didn't transmit it.

One afternoon, I was completing my final walkthrough of a property that we were about to open, reviewing the last details before the opening. The rooms were immaculate. The furniture was perfectly placed. The amenities sat precisely where they belonged. Everything aligned with the checklist. Yet the space felt strangely empty—as if something essential had not yet arrived. The physical space had no soul.

I stood still and let the silence speak. What was missing wasn't a detail or an object. It was an energy—the energy that comes when someone has infused themselves into the moment. Hospitality, I realized then, does not come alive through perfection of logistics. Hospitality comes alive through presence. Through care that is felt, not just executed.

And presence begins with awareness.

That moment in the suite became a mirror to the rest of my life. I saw the parallels everywhere: the way a hotel lobby and a living room both hold the emotional tone of the person entering; the way a team and a family both respond to the energy of their leader; the way attention, more than action, communicates priority.

Leadership isn't defined by how much we do.
Leadership is defined by how we show up while doing it.

As I deepened the practice of noticing, I began to feel another shift — subtle, but unmistakable. Awareness softened the edges of my reactivity. I found myself pausing before speaking, taking a breath before responding, observing the emotional state of a room before offering direction. I became more attuned to the energy within me and around me. Conversations became richer. Meetings unfolded with more clarity. Even the simplest interactions — greeting a team member, listening to my children, entering my home at the end of the day — felt more grounded.

But awareness alone was not enough. Awareness opened the door, but it also revealed a new responsibility: the responsibility to choose how I would use the space between stimulus and response.

That is where intention emerged — not as a grand declaration, but as a quiet form of self-leadership. Intention is what transforms noticing into creation. It is what shifts us from living unconsciously to living deliberately. It is what gives presence its power.

This is where the roots of Conscious Hospitality began to grow — not as a theory or a framework, but as a lived experience. I started to understand that if I wanted to lead others well, I first had to lead my attention. If I wanted to be a better father, I had to be fully present in the moments my children needed me. If I wanted to create connection, I had to bring the energy that made connection possible.

The question that began to echo through my days was deceptively simple:

"What would my life look like if I lived it fully present?"

Not occasionally.
Not when convenient.
Not as a performance.
But as a way of being.

Presence was not slowing down.
Presence was waking up.

And from that awakening, a deeper layer of inquiry began to take shape — one that would ultimately redefine how I understood leadership, energy, and human potential.

Awareness had opened the door.

Intention was preparing me to walk through it.

What came next was the *Conscious Shift* I referred to earlier—an inner turning point that transformed how I directed my attention, how I managed my energy, and how I stepped into responsibility with clarity and purpose.

And that shift would not only change my leadership—it would change my life.

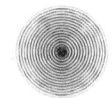

CHAPTER 3
The Conscious Shift

*"Until you make the unconscious conscious,
it will direct your life and you will call it fate."*

—Carl Jung

Awareness is the first step. But awareness alone does not create change. It opens the door; it does not walk us through it. After the initial awakening with my coach—after seeing with painful clarity how distracted I had become— there was a second revelation, quieter but just as profound: knowing I was distracted wasn't enough. I needed to understand *why* it happened so easily, *how* it shaped my life, and *what* it was costing me.

The journey from distraction to consciousness is not sudden. It unfolds in layers. At first, it shows you the surface: the habits, the reflexes, the compulsions. But if you sit with awareness long enough, it begins revealing what lies underneath: the stories, the beliefs, the conditioning, the fears, and the energy that fuel those behaviors.

As I continued noticing my days with greater honesty, patterns emerged— patterns that had been hiding in plain sight. My mornings began with my phone before my breath. My workdays were strung together by urgency instead of clarity. My evenings were scattered between conversations at home and unfinished loops in my mind. I convinced myself it was normal. That this was what responsibility looked like. That being responsive was the price of being effective. But as I watched myself with more presence, I saw a different truth: I had stopped choosing. I wasn't leading my attention; my attention was leading me.

For years, I moved through life as though I had no agency over my impulses. As though my phone, my calendar, my inbox, and the expectations of others dictated my behavior. But when I began observing my days with conscious awareness, something unexpected happened: I started seeing micro moments where I could have chosen differently. And if choice was available—even in the smallest moments—then distraction was not destiny. It was simply the default.

This realization emerged fully during a moment of extraordinary ordinariness. I was in the hallway of the hotel I was running, between two meetings, when a team member approached me. I remember the look on her face—uncertain, hesitant—something clearly weighing on her heart. She wanted to talk. I nodded, smiled politely, and gave her a quick answer before moving on. It took me all of three seconds. But as I walked away, something tugged at me. I felt a disconnect between the man I wanted to be and the way I had just shown up.

Presence had shown me the gap. Responsibility required addressing it.

Later that day, I began to reflect—not superficially, but deeply—on how often this happened. How often I gave half of myself to the people who deserved more. How often my attention was fragmented, even in moments that called for my full humanity. I saw that distraction was not merely a flaw of habit. It was a cultural force. A societal current. And I had been swimming with it for so long that I had forgotten there was a choice to swim differently.

My coach sensed this shift and guided me into the next phase of our work. If presence was the first awakening, then attention would become the second. She asked me to study my own energy with the same curiosity and rigor that I brought to any of my hotel projects. What were the forces pulling at me? What drained me? What nourished me? Where was I aligned, and where was I out of rhythm with myself?

At the same time, I was immersing myself in the teachings of Eckhart Tolle. I had read him years before, but the words had remained ideas. Now, they began landing in my body. Presence was not just awareness—it was alignment. It was the ability to inhabit this moment fully, without dragging the past behind me or leaning prematurely into the future. It was a discipline. A practice. A portal.

To deepen this integration, my coach introduced something she called an energetic activity study. The assignment was straightforward: track every activity, every interaction, every task—for a full forty-eight hours. For each one, I had to mark whether it energized me or drained me. No analysis. No justification. Just honest observation.

CALENDAR

MON	TUE	WED	THU	FRI	SAT	SUN
		ENERGIZING				
		DRAINING				

When I mapped the results, the truth was impossible to ignore. My energy had a rhythm—and I had been working against it for years. My peak focus hours were early morning and late afternoon, yet I often filled those windows with administrative tasks that depleted me. The meetings and conversations that fueled me were scattered throughout the day instead of intentionally placed. I realized that I had been managing my calendar based on urgency, not on energetic intelligence.

And then there was the screen-time data. When I finally looked, I felt a mix of embarrassment and clarity. Six hours and twenty-three minutes a day spent on my phone. Nearly three hours of that on social media—Instagram and LinkedIn. The rest divided between messages, emails, music, and consumption disguised as learning.

The numbers weren't just information. They were illumination. They revealed how easily I gave my attention away, how much energy bled through the cracks of unconscious habit, and how this fracturing of attention created a fracturing of presence.

For a moment, I felt shame—a heavy recognition that the man who valued consciousness had been operating unconsciously in the most basic rhythms of his day. But something else followed: empowerment. Because if I was responsible for creating the pattern, then I was also capable of changing it.

I took immediate action. I removed Instagram from my phone, choosing to access it only on desktop. I reorganized my calendar around my energetic highs and lows. I stopped scheduling back-to-back meetings that left no space for thought or breath. I began protecting my mornings, dedicating them to clarity and creation rather than reaction. Slowly, my days shifted from being something that happened to me into something I was actively shaping.

As I made these changes, I noticed something remarkable: when my attention came into coherence, so did my energy. My presence deepened. My patience expanded. The way I listened changed. Conversations with my team felt richer. Interactions with my children felt fuller. I found myself less reactive, more intentional, more attuned to the emotional signals in the spaces around me.

This is when a new understanding clicked into place—one that would become central to my philosophy of leadership:

WHERE YOU PLACE YOUR ATTENTION IS WHERE YOU PLACE YOUR ENERGY

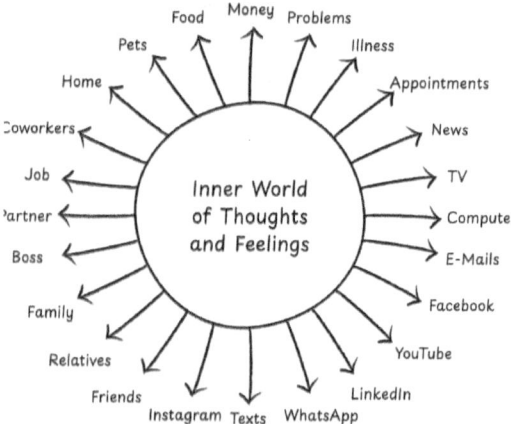

This wasn't just a concept from Joe Dispenza or a line repeated in spiritual circles. It was something I began witnessing in real time. Attention was not simply a cognitive function—it was a creative force. It shaped my emotions. It shaped my interactions. It shaped the energy I brought into rooms and the energy others brought back to me.

And that led to another realization—one that struck with the weight of responsibility:

If I had the ability to direct my attention, then I also had the responsibility to do so.

This was the Conscious Shift.

The moment I understood that agency was not about controlling everything. It was about choosing what I would amplify. It was about deciding what I would embody. It was about acknowledging that leadership begins with the sovereignty of one's own attention.

Agency is the right and the capacity to choose, in each and every moment.

And if I wanted to lead others—to inspire them, support them, elevate them—I first had to lead myself.

What surprised me most was that the shift didn't come through force. It came through gentleness. Through noticing without judgment. Through understanding without shame. Through choosing over and over again to come back to myself.

Every time I paused before reacting, I strengthened my awareness.
Every time I redirected my attention, I strengthened my intention.
Every time I aligned my actions with my inner state, I strengthened my consciousness.

This wasn't productivity. It wasn't time management. It was self-leadership.

And it began reshaping the way I moved through the world. Conversations with my team became more spacious. Solutions emerged more naturally. Meetings felt less like obligations and more like collaborative exchanges. Even my relationship with technology transformed—from compulsion to tool, from master to servant.

But the greatest transformation happened internally. My inner dialogue softened. My emotional regulation deepened. I began to feel myself more clearly: my tensions, my desires, my fears, my intuition. I began to distinguish between the noise of the ego and the truth of my energy.

This shift prepared me for what would come next. Because once I learned to direct my attention with intention, I began to see an even deeper force at play— one that would reshape my understanding of leadership, human behavior, and the emotional currents that connect us all.

If presence was the awakening, and attention was the shift, then energy would become the frontier.

This is where consciousness moved from concept to embodiment. Where leadership moved from behavior to resonance. Where the inner journey began transforming not only my decisions, but the frequency with which I met the world.

And that path—the path from ego to energy—would redefine everything. It would show me not just how to direct my attention, but how to align my entire being.

That journey begins in the next chapter.

CHAPTER 4

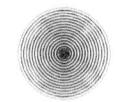

From Ego to Energy

*"Ego says: once everything falls into place, I will find peace.
Spirit says: find peace, and everything will fall into place."*

—Eckhart Tolle

Before I understood consciousness, I understood performance. Before I understood frequency, I understood force. And before I ever learned the language of energy, I was fluent in the language of ambition—first on the soccer field, then in luxury hospitality, and eventually in every role I held as a leader, husband, and father.

For much of my life, excellence meant intensity. Success meant visibility. Responsibility meant carrying weight. I chased outcomes the way I chased the ball as a teenager: with hunger, determination, and the belief that the harder I pushed, the more I deserved. In both soccer and hospitality, I loved the rush, the rhythm, the momentum of being in the center of everything. I loved the feeling of being counted on. And if I'm honest, I loved the validation that came with it even more.

There is a certain electricity in being seen, a certain energy in being praised, a certain thrill in being told you're needed, competent, exceptional. These sensations are not inherently wrong—they are deeply human. But they are seductive. They feed the ego in ways that feel like fuel, even as they slowly drain the deeper parts of us.

Hospitality became the stage on which my ego performed beautifully. The compliments, the guest letters, the promotions, the invitations to speak—all of it affirmed the image I crafted with such precision. I convinced myself this was leadership. That hyper-responsibility was a badge of honor. That stress was proof of dedication. That exhaustion was a natural price for excellence.

Yet beneath the surface, something was shifting. As presence returned to my life, I began noticing the gap between my outer success and my inner alignment. I was delivering results, but I was not creating resonance. I was advancing, but I was also hardening. I was present physically, but energetically distant. And something in me whispered that I could not keep living at this dissonance.

Awareness had revealed how my attention shattered into fragments. Intention showed me I could redirect that attention. But when I looked at the deeper patterns—what drove me, what shaped me, what I was still chasing—it became clear that distraction wasn't the only force pulling me away from myself. The ego was tugging at the strings too.

The ego is not an enemy. It is simply the part of us that seeks identity, safety, recognition, and control. It forms a narrative that helps us navigate the world. But when it becomes the director of our lives, its influence begins to distort what we feel, how we behave, and what we believe to be possible.

My own ego didn't show up as arrogance or superiority. It showed up as competence. As helpfulness. As the desire to be indispensable. I equated validation with worth, productivity with value, and constant motion with strength. From the outside, it looked like excellence. From the inside, it was fragility wrapped in ambition.

My coach helped me see this clearly. She asked questions that reached beneath my behaviors into the beliefs that fueled them. Why did I respond instantly to every message? Why did I fill every moment with activity? Why was silence uncomfortable? Why did I struggle to rest without guilt?

The answers revealed themselves in layers. I had built an identity around being necessary. Being admired. Being the one who delivered. My ego thrived on that narrative. But it also trapped me inside a loop of proving, performing, and producing. I was chasing an external version of success that satisfied everyone but me.

This is where the work deepened—not in my schedule or my habits, but in my energy.

Emotion is energy in motion. That simple sentence, which I first encountered through Joe Dispenza's teachings, changed the way I understood myself. Emotions are not cognitive puzzles to solve; they are frequencies that move through the body. They elevate or constrict. They open or protect. They flow or stagnate.

I began observing the emotional currents beneath my actions. Excitement carried warmth and openness. Anxiety contracted my breath. Gratitude expanded my chest. Anger surged with heat. And beneath many of these emotions lived something even deeper: fear. Fear of not being enough. Fear of failing. Fear of being unseen.

Avoiding these emotions didn't make them disappear. They would reappear through frustration, irritability, impatience, or withdrawal. The ego resisted them because they threatened its identity. But consciousness invited me to feel them—to let them speak, to let them move, and to let them guide me toward alignment.

This exploration accelerated dramatically when I discovered the Map of Consciousness developed by Dr. David R. Hawkins. What began as curiosity became a cornerstone of how I now understand leadership, energy, and human behavior. Hawkins mapped emotional states not as static labels but as vibrational frequencies, calibrated in a spectrum that offers profound insight into why humans act the way they do.

MAP OF CONSCIOUSNESS

	LEVEL	**EMOTION**
700+	ENLIGHTENMENT	Ineffable
600	PEACE	Bliss
540	JOY	Serenity
500	LOVE	Reverence
400	REASON	Understanding
350	ACCEPTANCE	Forgiveness
310	WILLINGNESS	Optimism
250	NEUTRALITY	Trust
200	COURAGE	Affirmation
175	PRIDE	Scorn
150	ANGER	Hate
125	DESIRE	Craving
100	FEAR	Anxiety
75	GRIEF	Regret
50	APATHY	Despair
30	GUILT	Blame
20	SHAME	Humiliation

At the lowest end of the scale are the states of contraction: shame, guilt, apathy, grief, fear. These are the energies of survival. They feel heavy because the body collapses inward, the nervous system goes into protection, and perception narrows. Anyone who has carried guilt or shame knows the weight these states impose. They anchor us in self-doubt and disconnect us from possibility.

Slightly higher on the scale are states like anger, desire, and pride. These are more active energies—energizing, mobilizing, and often socially rewarded. They drive competition, ambition, performance, and external achievement. I lived here for years. Pride fueled my confidence; desire fueled my ambition; anger fueled my resilience. These states helped me succeed, but they also kept me reactive, guarded, and subtly disconnected from my deeper truth.

The inflection point of the entire map is courage. At 200, courage marks the transition from living life reactively to living life consciously. Courage is not loud; it is steady. It is not arrogance; it is willingness. It is not force; it is honesty. Courage is the moment you stop hiding from yourself. It is where responsibility begins—not the heavy responsibility of burden, but the empowered responsibility of choice.

Above courage lie the expansive states of acceptance, love, joy, and peace. These are not passive emotions. They are powerful frequencies. Acceptance widens perception. Love opens the heart and creates safety. Joy amplifies creativity. Peace stabilizes presence. Leaders operating from these states don't motivate through pressure; they inspire through resonance. Their presence calms nervous systems, expands possibility, and creates environments where others can thrive.

Hawkins' map is not a hierarchy of moral worth. It is a mirror of energetic reality. Consciousness is fluid. We move up and down the scale throughout the day. We can be loving at work and fearful at home. Open in a morning meeting and contracted in an evening conversation. The map does not judge; it guides.

Once I began applying this framework to my leadership, everything shifted. I started asking myself: What frequency am I bringing into this moment? What energy am I transmitting before I speak? What state am I inviting others into—even without words?

Leadership is not just behavior. Leadership is transmission.

People respond to our energy long before they respond to our expertise. Teams synchronize with the nervous system of the leader. Families attune to the emotional state of the parent. Guests feel the presence of a host the moment they enter a space. Energy is the invisible architecture shaping human connection.

This became clear in moments that previously felt ordinary. Walking into a briefing with a scattered mind created tension in the room. Entering with calm created openness. Rushing through the door at home after a long day created fragmentation; arriving with intention softened everyone. My frequency was speaking louder than my words ever could.

To deepen this awareness, I developed a simple but transformative practice I call the Emotional Compass. It became a daily way of attuning to my state without judgment. I would pause and ask:

What am I feeling right now?
Where is it living in my body?
Can I breathe into it and allow it to move?
What is this emotion trying to tell me?

This practice taught me that emotions are not barriers to overcome but signals to follow. Anger pointed to crossed boundaries. Sadness asked for rest. Frustration revealed misalignment. Joy pointed toward authenticity. Friction showed me where I was living out of ego. Flow showed me where I was living in alignment.

Slowly, I began letting energy guide my leadership. I became less reactive and more responsive. Less defensive and more curious. Less performative and more authentic. My ambition didn't diminish—it matured. My drive didn't weaken—it recalibrated. My leadership didn't lessen—it deepened.

I stopped relying on force and began relying on frequency. I stopped chasing admiration and began cultivating alignment. I stopped performing worthiness and began living from presence.

This is the shift from ego to energy—the shift that changes not only how we lead, but who we are while leading.

Presence opened the doorway.
Attention created the shift.
Energy revealed the truth.

Together, these three awakenings formed the foundation of what would become the Conscious Hospitality Framework.

INTEGRATION

EMPATHY

INTENTION

AUTHENTICITY

PRESENCE

With this foundation set, we now transition from the personal journey into the practical application—from inner transformation to outer leadership. The next part of the book explores exactly how to bring this awareness into your daily life, your teams, your family, and the spaces you serve.

PART II
THE CONSCIOUS HOSPITALITY FRAMEWORK

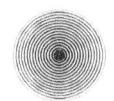

CHAPTER 5
Presence: The Foundational Portal

"The present moment is the only time over which we have dominion."
—Thich Nhat Hanh

Presence is where everything begins—and where everything returns. It is not a concept or a technique. It is not a leadership hack or a productivity tool. Presence is a state, a frequency, a way of being in your body, in your breath, in your life. It is the foundation of Conscious Hospitality because without presence, nothing else—authenticity, intention, empathy—can truly take root. You can have the right strategy, the right systems, the right brand language, but if you are not there when it matters, people will feel the absence before they see the effort.

The moment I began exploring presence was the moment everything shifted, both at home and at work.

It started with a simple, piercing question from the coach who had been guiding me after my 360-degree feedback and the moment with Cruz:

"How do you behave when you enter a sacred place? A temple? A church? A synagogue?"

Even if you are not religious, there is a natural softening that happens when you cross such thresholds. You lower your voice. Your steps slow. You notice the space around you. You bring reverence—not because someone hands you a manual, but because the space invites it. The atmosphere itself shapes your behavior.

She paused, looked at me, and added:

"Why don't you treat your home like that? Isn't that where everything you care about actually lives?"

Those words landed like a stone dropping into still water. They revealed a truth I hadn't yet seen: I had been treating my home like an extension of my to-do list—physically present, but energetically absent. I walked through the door with my mind still racing through emails, problems, deadlines. The sacredness of people, moments, laughter, and connection was all being overlooked. My home was a temple I kept entering as if it were a corridor.

That realization did not shame me; it awakened me. It was the beginning of a new kind of awareness—one that wasn't about fixing distractions or checking more boxes, but about *being* differently: more grounded, more attuned, more present. Presence stopped being a concept; it began to reveal itself as a way of orienting myself to the world.

The coach gave me tools—meditation, journaling, breathwork, and what she called "awareness in motion:" the practice of presence not only in quiet reflection, but while life is unfolding in real time. Slowly, almost imperceptibly at first, these practices began to reshape the way I inhabited my body, my mind, and my relationships.

Before you can manage people, you must manage your nervous system. Before you can cultivate culture, you must anchor yourself in your body. Before you can lead others, you must lead your own breath.

Your breath is the remote control of your nervous system. You cannot always control your environment, but you can always return to your breath. Most people breathe shallowly, unconsciously, restrictively—a reflection of their emotional state. When fear or stress kicks in, the breath becomes short and tight. When we're overwhelmed, we often hold our breath without realizing it. The inverse is also true: when we breathe with intention, we can shift our emotional and physiological state in seconds.

Breath is how the body tells the brain, I'm safe now. It is how we reclaim the present moment, regulate our heart rate, and reset the nervous system. In a world that is overstimulated, over-caffeinated, and under-rested, breath may be the most underused tool of leadership.

Our autonomic nervous system has two primary branches. The sympathetic nervous system prepares us for "fight or flight"—activated by threat, urgency, or performance pressure. The parasympathetic nervous system supports rest, restoration, and digestion—activated by safety, connection, and presence. Most people in leadership or service roles live in chronic sympathetic overdrive. Constant urgency. Constant reactivity. Always "on." The result is predictable: anxiety, fatigue, short tempers, shallow empathy, and a steep decline in creativity, intuition, and long-term thinking.

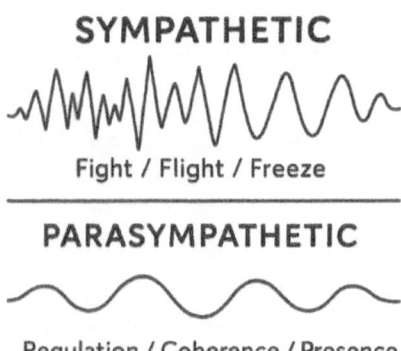

SYMPATHETIC

Fight / Flight / Freeze

PARASYMPATHETIC

Regulation / Coherence / Presence

When you breathe slowly and deeply, especially with longer exhales, you signal the parasympathetic system to step in. This is how we shift from reactivity to response, from contraction to expansion, from frantic urgency to grounded action.

If breath is the anchor, movement is the unlock. Emotion is energy in motion; when it gets stuck, the body becomes a storage unit for stress, grief, fear, and unprocessed experience. When you move — walk, stretch, dance, flow — you allow that energy to be expressed and released. You give yourself permission to feel. You clear the system.

This isn't about aesthetics or gym metrics. This is about embodiment. A regulated body leads to a regulated mind. A regulated leader becomes a stabilizing presence for the entire team.

Your team may smile at you. Guests may nod politely. But your body will always tell you the truth. Are your shoulders tense or relaxed? Is your jaw clenched? Are your feet grounded or constantly pacing? Is your breath flowing freely? Are you even aware of your body right now?

Most of us were taught to lead from the neck up. Yet the greatest leaders I have met have a grounded presence that begins at the feet. They move slowly. They breathe deeply. They take up space not through dominance, but through coherence. They embody what others are craving.

Eckhart Tolle's *The Power of Now* gave me language for what I was beginning to experience: everything exists only in the present moment. Not in the anxiety of the imagined future. Not in the heaviness of the remembered past. Only here, now. He writes that what is truly precious is not time itself, but the timeless point we call the "Now." I realized I did not need to escape to a monastery to find it. I simply had to pay attention.

Presence became how I walked through the door. How I brewed my coffee. How I transitioned between meetings. How I spoke to my wife. How I played with my children. The temple was no longer outside of me. It was everywhere.

Most of us already practice presence in small, unconscious ways. I used to lie down with my children at night and rub their backs in the simple rhythm we called "criss-cross applesauce." I would intentionally calm my energy so they could fall asleep more easily. It was one of the first moments where I truly felt the power of stillness. Something in me slowed and softened. Something in them responded.

Even making coffee in the morning can become a portal. When done slowly and with full attention—measuring the beans, grinding, listening to the kettle, pouring the water—it becomes more than routine. It becomes a ritual of arrival. A moment of reverence. A return to now. Presence doesn't mean pausing your life; it means being in it, fully.

You feel presence when you look someone in the eyes and truly see them. When you choose not to pick up your phone at the dinner table. When you take a single conscious breath before responding to something that triggers you. Earlier in this book, we explored Viktor Frankl's idea that between stimulus and response there is a space. Presence is what expands that space. In that expansion lies our freedom.

Modern neuroscience now confirms what mystics have suggested for centuries: the quality of your attention determines the quality of your life. The prefrontal cortex, which handles decision-making, focus, and planning, is constantly negotiating with the limbic brain, which craves dopamine, novelty, and escape. We live in an attention economy. Your focus is the most valuable asset you own, and almost everything around you is designed to pull it away from the present moment. Presence is how you take it back.

It is not only about turning off notifications. It is about noticing when your mind wanders, when you leave the moment, when you rehearse conversations or replay old wounds. It is about gently returning your awareness from past and future into the only place where any change can happen: right now.

When you live primarily in the future, anxiety grows—but so can hope. When you live primarily in the past, sorrow deepens—but so can gratitude and learning. When you live in the present, you have the power to choose which story you feed. Much of our reactivity—whether in leadership, parenting, or daily life—does not come from logic. It comes from a nervous system that is overstimulated and under-supported. When your system is dysregulated, your window of tolerance shrinks. You become quick to anger, prone to shutdown, or hypersensitive to stress.

Presence expands that window. It allows you to notice the tightness before you yell. The withdrawal before you disappear. The judgment before it takes over. It offers you one sacred breath where a different path becomes available.

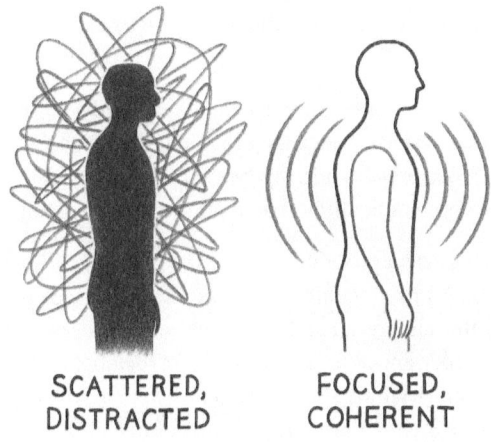

SCATTERED, DISTRACTED   FOCUSED, COHERENT

Time is a construct we use to give structure to our days. Presence is not bound by it. Presence is the experience of being fully where you are, with what is, as it is. It gives you access to your true power: the power to choose your next thought, your next action, your next energetic imprint.

One of the most important realizations I had was that true presence isn't rigid— it's responsive. It's not about forcing stillness for the sake of appearing calm. It's about developing the inner flexibility to meet each moment exactly as it is. Presence, in its purest form, is adaptability in motion. When you are present, you're no longer broadcasting a fixed signal; you're attuned to a wider range of frequencies. You can sense what's needed, who's hurting, what is alive in the space around you. You become more available, more human.

In physics, there is a notion of coherence: different elements aligning into a harmonious pattern. Presence creates coherence. It expands your bandwidth. In leadership, that means you can connect with more people in more ways, without forcing them to meet you where you are. Instead, you meet them where they are. In doing so, you create trust, safety, and resonance.

If you are not present as a leader, you are creating a culture of disconnection. Your team feels it. Your guests feel it. Your children feel it. Presence is energetic. You walk into a room and your frequency speaks before you do. Are you scattered or grounded? Distracted or attentive? Closed or available? Remember what we explored in the previous chapter: through the lens of the Map of Consciousness, your state of being determines the frequency you radiate. Presence lifts that frequency into coherence.

As I was starting to embody this practice, another experience changed my life forever.

Sanctum—a mindful movement experience created by Luuk Melisse and Gabriel Olszewski—arrived at exactly the right time. I didn't seek it; it found me. I knew it blended breathwork, rhythm, somatic movement, and spirituality, but I had no idea how radically it would alter my internal landscape.

The first class was deceptively simple: slow music, deliberate breathing, gentle grounding. And yet, within minutes, something inside me began to shift. It bypassed my thinking mind and spoke directly to my nervous system. For the first time, I experienced presence not as an idea but as a physical reality. My breath became rhythm. My movement became prayer. The energy of the room became a mirror, showing the parts of myself I had left unattended.

I was not leading. I was not performing. I was not in control. I was simply alive in my body.

Tears surfaced—not from sadness, but from release, from recognition, from remembering. Through Sanctum, I understood something I had never truly grasped on the soccer field, in the boardroom, or in a luxury lobby: the body is not just a vehicle for consciousness; it is a gateway to it.

As the sessions continued, I learned to stay with my breath even as intensity rose. I allowed emotion to move through me without fearing collapse. I expanded my nervous system's capacity for presence. I softened without losing strength. I held power without force. Alignment became a living, breathing experience rather than a concept.

Awareness had revealed the problem; embodiment offered the solution. It was no longer enough to notice my distraction. I had to feel my presence. I had to inhabit it fully. I had to reclaim my energy and, with it, my agency.

From that point onward, every interaction—whether with a guest, a colleague, or my children—carried a new quality. Presence became the lens through which I led, parented, and lived. When breath, body, and attention aligned, presence became a living force. It regulated rooms without a word. It steadied conversations without control. It transformed crises into opportunities for coherence.

Presence lives in small, ordinary, easily overlooked moments—the way you step through a door, the way you greet a team member, the way you sit down at the dinner table. It is not a posture; it is a practice. A discipline. A commitment to returning to yourself, again and again, even when the world pulls you away.

I began noticing these micro-moments of choice. Walking into my home after a long day, I would feel my shoulders still carrying the weight of work, my jaw still clenched, my mind still spinning. In the past, I would have walked straight in, bringing that energy into the living room. Now, I paused at the threshold. One breath. Then another. A conscious decision: I am here now. I would step in differently. My children felt the difference immediately, even if they couldn't name it.

The body was always speaking first. Shoulders tightening, heart racing, feet pacing—these were whispers of the nervous system, signaling whether I was operating from alignment or from reactive habit. It was astonishing how much energy I had been leaking simply by not listening to my own physiology before stepping into a room.

The autonomic nervous system became my first teacher. In hospitality, I saw its effects constantly. When I entered a team briefing frazzled from a previous crisis, the energy of the room mirrored me. Voices were clipped, ideas tentative, creativity shut down. Guests sensed it too—the rushed steps, the slightly sharp tone, the forced smile.

During one pre-opening, our IT systems failed catastrophically just days before launch. Weeks of preparation evaporated in a moment. The anxiety in the room was thick. My first impulse was to escalate, to command, to inject more urgency. Instead, I remembered what I had been learning. I paused. I breathed. I grounded myself before I spoke.

The shift in the room was tangible. Fear softened into focus. Frantic chatter gave way to clear thinking. We still had a serious problem to solve, but we were solving it from courage instead of panic. Presence had created a container where coherence could emerge.

Calm energy, I learned, is more effective than frantic action. Leadership is first about regulating energy, then about directing effort.

The same truth appeared at home. On days when I returned wired and scattered, small frustrations escalated quickly. When I returned regulated and present, conflicts dissolved more easily, and laughter returned sooner. My presence— or lack of it—was the emotional thermostat. The Map of Consciousness helped me name what I was feeling: Was I operating from fear and frustration, or from courage and love? The answer showed up in my body long before it showed up in my words.

Even the smallest acts became laboratories for presence. One breath before responding to a question. A deliberate pause before giving feedback. Noticing the subtle shift in someone's posture when I entered the room. Each of these moments reinforced the feedback loop between nervous system regulation, energy coherence, and conscious leadership.

Presence also revealed cultural nuances. In Hong Kong, I once opened a meeting by asking a large group, "How is everyone doing?" Silence filled the room. I realized later that the question, though common in Western contexts, created discomfort in that particular setting. Energy is read before words. Presence requires attunement not only to oneself, but to the cultural and emotional landscape of others.

Over time, presence stopped being something I did and became something I carried. It was dynamic, not static—an ongoing calibration to each moment, person, and environment. It transformed ordinary actions into rituals, interactions into trust, spaces into containers of safety.

At this point in the journey, presence can no longer stay as an inspiring idea on the page. It must move from theory into practice—into your breath, your body, your calendar, your conversations. What follows is an invitation to you. This is where you begin to do the work.

PRACTICES OF PRESENCE

1. The Threshold Pause

Before entering any space—your home, office, a meeting room—pause for a brief moment.

- Take three slow, conscious breaths.
- Feel your feet on the ground and the weight of your body.
- Silently set an intention: "I enter this space with presence. I bring calm, clarity, and attention."

Notice how different the room feels when you walk in having already grounded yourself.

2. The One-Minute Reset

Several times a day, give yourself sixty seconds.

- Stop whatever you are doing.
- Close your eyes if possible and scan your body.
- Notice your breath, your posture, any tension or agitation.

Inhale gently, exhale slowly, and allow yourself to return to the present moment. These small resets act like tiny recalibrations for your nervous system.

3. Walking Presence

Choose one walk each day—however short—and dedicate it to pure presence.

- Leave your phone in your pocket or at home.
- Feel each step. Notice the contact of your feet with the ground.
- Observe sounds, smells, colors, textures around you.

Let your awareness widen beyond thought and into sensation.

Walking becomes meditation in motion, bringing your mind back into your body.

4. Eye Contact Ritual

Once a day, in a conversation with a child, partner, friend, or team member, practice full presence.

- Put away distractions.
- Look the other person in the eyes and really see them.
- Listen not just for words, but for tone, emotion, and energy.

Presence deepens connection long before solutions or advice enter the conversation.

5. Presence in Conflict

The next time tension rises—an email that irritates you, a comment that stings, a child acting out—experiment with a pause.

- Take one conscious breath before you react.
- Feel the surge of emotion in your body.
- Ask yourself: "Do I want to react from this state, or respond from presence?"

Even a three-second pause can turn a repeated pattern into a new possibility.

6. Evening Presence Scan

Before bed, spend a few minutes revisiting your day.

- Where did you feel truly present?
- Where were you distracted, scattered, or shut down?
- What moments would you like to meet differently tomorrow?

This is not about criticism; it is about building the muscle of self-observation.

7. Movement & Breath Alignment

Schedule at least one short session of conscious movement each day: stretching, yoga, dancing, or simply moving your body with your breath.

- Let your breath guide the movement—inhale as you expand, exhale as you release.
- Notice how your mental state shifts as your body moves.

When breath and movement align, presence becomes embodied rather than theoretical.

8. Sanctum-Inspired Practice

Set aside ten minutes to combine breath, music, and movement.

- Choose a track that makes you feel alive.
- Close your eyes, breathe deeply, and let your body move intuitively.
- Notice what emotions arise and allow them to pass through without judgment.

This practice reconnects you with aliveness and reminds your body what presence feels like.

9. Energy Audit

At three points during the day—morning, midday, evening—pause and ask:

- What energy am I carrying right now?
- How might it be affecting the people around me?
- What small adjustment in breath, posture, or focus could bring me back into coherence?

Over time, this awareness turns presence into a continuous feedback loop between your inner state and outer impact.

REFLECTION: ANCHORING AWARENESS

These questions are invitations, not exams. Take your time with them. They are meant to deepen your self-observation and gently widen the space between stimulus and response.

- Where in my daily life do I most often notice myself drifting away from the present moment—during transitions, meals, meetings, commutes, or family time?
- When was the last time I felt fully, undeniably present? What conditions made that possible?
- Who in my life receives the most "absent" version of me? Who gets my leftovers instead of my full attention?
- What types of triggers pull me out of presence—criticism, urgency, boredom, rejection, over-stimulation?
- Where in my body do I feel contraction most strongly? Where do I feel expansion? How do these sensations correlate with specific people, environments, or tasks?

- If my presence were a frequency that others could hear, what would it sound like today? What would I like it to sound like tomorrow?

Write your reflections down. Presence strengthens each time you are honest with yourself about where you are and how you are showing up.

DO THE WORK: EMBEDDING PRESENCE

These simple practices help translate insight into integration. Choose one or two to focus on for the next week, then layer in more as they become natural.

1. Presence Audit

Set three reminders on your phone — morning, afternoon, evening — with the question: "Am I present right now?" When it rings, answer honestly. If the answer is no, take one small step toward yes: a breath, a pause, a quick scan of your body.

2. Presence Partnership

Share your intention to cultivate presence with a trusted colleague, partner, or friend. Agree to check in with each other at the end of each day for one week:

- "Where were you present today?"
- "Where did you drift?"

Naming it together normalizes the journey and dissolves shame.

3. Sacred Space Challenge

Choose one space in your home or workplace — a corner, a chair, a small area — and declare it "sacred ground."

- Keep it tidy.
- Enter it with intention.

Use it for moments of breath, reflection, or recalibration. Over time, your body will begin to associate that space with presence.

4. Micro-Moment Awareness

For one day, before answering any call, email, or message, take one conscious breath. Notice how this micro-pause changes your tone, your word choice, and your emotional state.

5. Embodied Observation

Spend a day simply observing how your presence affects others.

- How do people respond when you are grounded versus when you are rushed?
- What happens to group energy when you enter the room regulated versus scattered?

Do not judge—just notice. Awareness is the beginning of change.

Through these practices, presence ceases to be a beautiful idea and becomes a lived experience. It moves from your mind into your muscles, your breath, your calendar, your relationships. It becomes the quiet power you carry into every space—a power that regulates rather than reacts, that creates safety rather than stress, that opens doors rather than closes hearts.

As the weeks of practicing presence accumulated, I began to notice something profound: my life was no longer moving through me—it was moving *with* me. I was no longer swept along by the currents of distraction, urgency, or expectation. My energy, my attention, my awareness were anchored, grounded, and available. I could feel the subtle shifts in how people responded—not just in their words, but in the energy they carried, the way they entered spaces, the way moments unfolded. Presence had become more than a practice; it had become a way of being.

And yet, I quickly realized that being present was only the beginning. I could show up in every moment, fully attentive, fully embodied, and still not show up as myself. Presence opened the door, but it did not decide what—or who— walked through it. In some ways, showing up without authenticity is like standing in a beautiful room with all the lights on but keeping the blinds drawn. People see your outline, your posture, your effort, but they do not feel your essence.

Presence is the foundation. Authenticity is the expression. Presence allows you to inhabit the now. Authenticity allows the now to carry your truth. Without authenticity, presence is still filtered, moderated, diluted. Without presence, authenticity cannot land; it drifts, untethered, unanchored.

It was only when I began pairing my cultivated presence with a courageous willingness to show up as myself—without masks, without performance, without the compulsion to please—that I started to see transformation at a deeper level. Teams responded not just to my attention, but to my honesty.

Guests experienced not only care, but sincerity. My family began to mirror the energy I embodied rather than simply reacting to the version of me they expected.

In the next chapter, we will explore authenticity—the act of showing up as who you truly are. We will see how the nervous-system practices of presence prepare the soil, and how authenticity plants the seeds that allow trust, alignment, and resonance to flourish. Authenticity is the return to your frequency, the bridge between being and doing, the compass that directs the energy of every interaction.

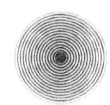

CHAPTER 6

Authenticity:
The Return to Your Frequency

"The privilege of a lifetime is to become who you truly are."

—Carl Jung

If presence is the act of showing up in the moment, authenticity is the act of showing up as yourself. But what does that really mean in a world shaped by expectations, unconscious conditioning, and constant pressure to perform?

From the moment we are born, we begin learning how to fit in, how to be liked, how to stay safe. Don Miguel Ruiz calls this process "domestication"—the slow shaping of our instincts to please, perform, and hide our truth. We learn what earns praise and what invites criticism. We learn which parts of us are celebrated and which are inconvenient. Over time, we trade small pieces of our essence for approval, comfort, status, or belonging.

As children, that trade is often unconscious and understandable. We depend on our caregivers for survival, so we adapt. We smile when we feel sad. We say yes when our body wants to say no. We learn to read the emotional weather of a room and adjust ourselves accordingly. Gabor Maté describes this tension as the lifelong dance between authenticity and attachment: when forced to choose, the child will sacrifice authenticity to preserve connection, because survival depends on it. If that pattern is never revisited in adulthood, we carry it into our families, our workplaces, and our leadership.

Science confirms what wisdom traditions have long intuited. Neuroscientists studying social conformity have found that the brain actively suppresses certain impulses to align with group expectations. The prefrontal cortex inhibits authentic responses so that we can adapt to the group and avoid rejection. Our nervous system literally trains itself to prioritize acceptance over truth. After years of repetition, suppression stops feeling like suppression. It just feels like being "professional," "polite," or "appropriate."

I felt this deeply in my early career.

When I arrived at Four Seasons Lanai, I came with the full momentum of my ego: my experience, my reputation, my desire to prove that I belonged among the best. I moved fast. I made decisive decisions. I restructured teams. I issued directives. Outwardly, it looked like leadership—strong, confident, effective. Inwardly, it felt hollow.

There were frozen smiles in the corridors, polite silence in meetings, and a noticeable absence of honest feedback. People complied, but they did not open. They followed instructions, but they did not bring their full selves. I told myself this was just the cost of high performance, but my body knew otherwise. I felt a tightness in my chest after certain conversations, a dull heaviness after team meetings, an unspoken distance between myself and the local team. Something in me knew I was acting a part rather than inhabiting myself.

I was leading from performance, not from presence. I was acting, not being.

The turning point did not arrive through confrontation, but through invitation. My general manager—who could easily have criticized or sidelined me— instead sent me to a sister property on another island for three days. Not as punishment, but as guidance. "Go observe," he said. "Go learn. Go listen."

What I encountered there was not a new strategy, but a different frequency.

I immersed myself in the local culture, observing what people call the "Aloha Spirit." Leaders greeted one another by name, not title. Morning briefings began with genuine check-ins rather than immediate to-do lists. Decisions were made slowly, with an ear for impact on people and community. The land was spoken about with reverence. There was no rush to prove. No need to dominate the conversation. No subtle competition for credit. Just presence.

In that environment, I became acutely aware of my own patterns. I noticed how performance had replaced presence, how ego had become my compass instead of truth. The contrast was uncomfortable and liberating at the same time. I realized that authenticity is not about trying to be good; it is about returning to who you already are beneath the performance.

When I returned to Lanai, I did not change everything overnight. But I began to test a different way of being.

I slowed down.
I asked more questions than I answered.

I listened to the stories behind the resistance.

I paid attention to body language, silence, and what was *not* being said.

Instead of imposing structures and expecting people to adapt, I started by aligning myself—my values, my energy, my intentions—with the culture I was there to serve. The results followed, but they were no longer the primary metric. Trust blossomed slowly, then all at once. People began to share ideas more freely. Resistance softened. The culture shifted from politeness to partnership. Presence remained the baseline; authenticity became the compass.

Psychology supports what I witnessed. Research on leadership from Brené Brown and others shows that vulnerability and authenticity increase trust, engagement, and collaboration. When leaders are willing to be human—to admit mistakes, to share uncertainty, to name what they truly care about—they create psychological safety. People no longer have to spend energy managing impressions; they can use that energy to create, serve, and grow.

Authenticity, at its core, is alignment. It is the harmony between what you feel, what you believe, what you say, and what you do. Carl Rogers, one of the pioneers of humanistic psychology, called this "congruence"—the inner and outer selves matching. When you are congruent, your nervous system relaxes. Your words and your energy tell the same story. People sense it immediately, even if they cannot explain why.

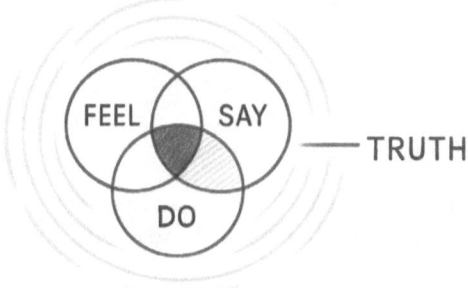

In contrast, inauthenticity is insidious. It does not always look dramatic. It seeps quietly into your posture, your breath, and your energy. You say you're fine while your jaw is clenched. You smile while your gut tightens. You agree in meetings while disagreeing in silence. Over time, these tiny fractures of truth manifest as tension, fatigue, fragmentation, and resentment. The cost is both emotional and physical.

I saw this clearly when I was assisting with the opening of a resort. On the surface, everything looked flawless. The team showed up polished and prepared—uniforms perfectly ironed, posture attentive, procedures memorized word for word. All the operational pieces were in place. Technically, we were ready to open the doors.

But energetically, something was off.

From the first moments of guest arrival, I felt it—a subtle dullness in the atmosphere, the absence of that unmistakable buzz that defines true hospitality. The staff were there in body but not in spirit. Greetings landed, but without warmth. Smiles appeared, but without spark. Conversations were polite, but empty of genuine human connection.

Guests sensed it immediately. Not because anything went wrong, but because nothing *felt* right.

Service boxes were checked, but the soul of hospitality was missing. Movements were precise but mechanical. Interactions were efficient but lifeless. The team followed the script perfectly, but hospitality is not meant to be scripted. It is meant to be lived.

Meetings during that period were equally telling—productive, well structured, but flat. There was no heartbeat, no sense of shared purpose. It became obvious: performance without authenticity creates a culture that is technically functional but emotionally dead.

That opening taught me something essential:
You cannot create resonance through standards alone.
You cannot force a culture into vibrancy.
You cannot operationalize spirit.

Authenticity had to come first—from the leaders, from the team, from the collective energy we chose to bring into the space.

Only then could the experience come alive.

Studies in psychophysiology show that chronic misalignment between internal state and outward behavior increases cortisol levels, contributing to stress, burnout, and cognitive depletion. Every forced smile, softened opinion, or withheld question taxes the nervous system. The more you perform a version of yourself that is not true, the more energy you must spend maintaining the mask.

Authenticity is most visible under pressure—during operational crises, difficult conversations, or moments of deep fatigue. When stress rises, the nervous system either amplifies the alignment you have cultivated or exposes the misalignment you have been hiding. Under pressure, pretending becomes harder. Your frequency reveals itself.

I recall a guest arrival one day that was fraught with tension. There had been a booking discrepancy involving a very important guest. The staff were anxious. My instinct, conditioned by years of performance, was to "fix it fast," to move quickly and decisively so no one would question my competence. But as I began to stride toward the lobby, I felt it—tightness in my chest, shallow breathing, a subtle internal rush.

Presence had taught me to notice those signals. I paused. A deep inhale. A slow exhale. A quiet question: "What energy do I want to bring here? Who do I choose to be in this moment?" I chose calm, clarity, and genuine care before I chose action.

When I stepped into the interaction from that place, everything shifted. The guest's shoulders softened when they saw my grounded demeanor. I apologized sincerely, without defensiveness. I listened fully before proposing solutions. The team, watching closely, began to mirror the steadiness rather than the stress. Emotional contagion—the phenomenon where people unconsciously mimic the emotions and nervous system states of others— was happening in real time. Authenticity was not just a moral idea; it was a stabilizing field shaping the entire room.

The same principles applied at home. When I arrived from work physically present but emotionally absent, small disagreements quickly flared into arguments. The kids reacted to the tension beneath my words, not the words themselves. Once I began pausing at the threshold, centering myself, and aligning my energy before stepping into the house, the rhythm shifted. Calm became contagious. Presence became coherent. Our home began to feel less like another "project" and more like a sanctuary again.

Sanctum deepened this understanding in a way that bypassed intellect. The combination of breath, posture, movement, and rhythm anchored my energy in truth. During intense sequences, I could hear the old voices of performance whispering: "Push harder. Prove more. Don't stop." But my body knew better. Authenticity in that context meant respecting my limits, honoring my actual state rather than the one my ego wanted to project. That simple act—choosing honesty over performance in movement—translated directly into my leadership. I began to notice where I was still pretending to be "fine," "strong," or "in control" when I was anything but.

You cannot lead authentically if you are fragmented, distracted, or constantly overriding your own signals. Your nervous system and your values must be in dialogue. The Map of Consciousness from the previous chapter comes into play here, too: authenticity requires courage—the level where we stop hiding from ourselves. To be authentic is to choose truth over image, even when it costs us short-term comfort. It is to move up the scale from fear and pride into willingness, acceptance, and eventually love.

Every small gesture—genuine eye contact, a conscious pause before answering, noticing a team member's nonverbal cues, admitting "I don't know" when you truly don't—became a micro-practice of authentic leadership. Over time, these micro-returns to alignment created a network of resonance that shaped culture more powerfully than any slogan or standard operating procedure.

Neuroplasticity research tells us that repeated conscious practices literally rewire the brain. Each time you interrupt a pattern of performance and choose authenticity instead, you carve a new pathway. Each time you speak a gentle truth instead of a polished answer, your nervous system learns that honesty can be safe. Over months and years, this is how authenticity stops being an aspiration and becomes a habit.

Authenticity is cultivated through repeated, conscious actions. It is not about perfection. It is about returning, again and again, to alignment with your true self—especially when it would be easier to perform.

And now, as with presence, this is the moment where the chapter turns toward you. Authenticity cannot be understood from the outside; it must be lived from the inside. The following practices and reflections are an invitation to explore what alignment means in your own life, in your leadership, and in your hospitality—to yourself and to others.

PRACTICES OF AUTHENTICITY

1. The Alignment Pause

Before entering any significant space—your home after work, a team meeting, a one-on-one conversation—pause.

- Take three conscious breaths.
- Notice your posture, your facial expression, the tension in your body.
- Ask yourself: "Who am I choosing to be here? What truth wants to come with me into this moment?"

Enter the space only when your inner state and your intention feel aligned.

2. Micro-Returns

During the day, begin to catch small moments of performance:

- Laughing when something isn't funny.
- Saying "yes" when your whole body wants to say "no."
- Nodding along when you internally disagree.

Each time you notice, pause. Breathe. Softly adjust course—even if the adjustment is internal at first. These micro-returns train you to come back to yourself without drama or self-judgment.

3. Truthful Expression

Once a day, practice speaking one simple, honest sentence that you might normally soften or avoid. It might be:

- "I actually see this differently."
- "I'm feeling tired today."
- "I'm not comfortable with that decision."
- "I'd love some help."

Observe how your body feels after speaking. Notice the impact on the relationship. This is not about being blunt or harsh; it is about letting your inner reality have a voice.

4. Boundaries in Action

Identify one situation where you habitually override yourself—taking on extra work, answering messages late at night, saying yes to social plans when you are depleted.

- Choose one small boundary to set this week.
- Communicate it clearly and kindly.
- Notice how your energy changes when you honor it.

Boundaries are not walls; they are the architecture that protects authenticity.

5. Intentional Presence in Relationships

During conversations with your partner, children, colleagues, or guests, observe your energy.

- Are you listening to understand or to respond?
- Are you saying what you think you "should" say, or what feels true?
- Is your body open or subtly defended?

Without trying to fix everything at once, choose one interaction each day to meet with full, aligned presence.

REFLECTION: ANCHORING AUTHENTICITY

Use these prompts as invitations into deeper self-honesty. Write your answers without editing yourself for what sounds "right." Let them be real.

- When today did I act from ego, obligation, or fear rather than from truth?
- Where did I feel subtle tension in my body that might have been a signal of inauthenticity?
- In which situations do I most often shape-shift—saying what is expected rather than what is true for me?
- Who around me receives the most "performed" version of me? What am I afraid would happen if I showed them more of who I truly am?
- Where in my life does my energy feel most aligned with my values? Where is there a noticeable gap?
- If my younger self could watch me lead today, what would they recognize as true—and what would feel like a performance?

These reflections are not here to judge you. They are here to illuminate where you are already aligned and where your system is asking for a kinder, truer way of being.

DO THE WORK: EMBEDDING AUTHENTICITY

The following practices help move authenticity from insight into habit. Choose one or two to begin with and let them integrate before adding more.

1. Alignment Audit

Set three daily reminders—morning, midday, evening—with the question: "Am I acting from truth right now?" When the reminder appears, take a brief inventory:

- What am I doing?
- How does my body feel?
- Is there anything I am pretending not to know or not to feel?

If misalignment is present, choose one tiny step toward truth—a breath, a boundary, an honest sentence, or a simple "I need a moment."

2. Presence and Authenticity Partnership

Invite a trusted colleague, friend, or partner into this work with you. For one week, share with each other at the end of the day:

- One moment you were proud of your authenticity.
- One moment you noticed yourself performing.
- One small adjustment you want to try tomorrow.

Mutual witnessing reduces shame and reinforces that everyone is learning.

3. Micro-Moment Awareness

For an entire day, before responding to any message, call, or request, take one conscious breath and silently ask: "What would be the most honest response here?" This does not mean you always say everything you think, but it ensures that your response is chosen rather than automatic.

4. Sacred Space for Truth

Choose one physical space—a chair, a corner of a room, a park bench— and designate it as your authenticity spot.

- When you sit there, commit to telling yourself the truth.
- Use it for journaling, decision-making, or simply checking in with how you really feel.

Over time, your nervous system will associate that space with safety and honesty.

5. Embodied Observation

For several days, turn your attention to how your authenticity affects others.

- How do people's faces, posture, and tone change when you speak from alignment rather than from performance?
- What happens in meetings when you admit uncertainty instead of pretending to know?
- How do your children or loved ones respond when you are honest about being tired, joyful, or worried?

Simply observe. Let reality teach you that authenticity, more often than not, deepens connection rather than breaking it.

Authenticity, as you can feel, is not a single breakthrough moment. It is a thread woven through the small choices of daily leadership and daily life. Each micro-return to truth—each moment you choose coherence over performance—reverberates outward. It strengthens your nervous system, refines your frequency on the Map of Consciousness, and allows your presence to carry real weight in ways that titles, scripts, or authority never can.

But authenticity alone, while essential, is only part of the equation. Presence without direction can float, untethered. Alignment without movement can remain inert. You can be deeply yourself and still drift if your energy has no channel.

This is where intention enters—the conscious fuel behind action, the unseen current that transforms presence and authenticity into purposeful impact. In the next chapter, we will explore how intention shapes the invisible architecture of leadership, infusing every decision, every interaction, every gesture with deliberate energy. It is here that the principles of conscious leadership and hospitality converge, moving beyond "being" into "doing with purpose," turning awareness into a force that shapes not only outcomes, but the lived experience of everyone you serve.

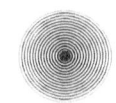

CHAPTER 7

Intention:
The Fuel of Conscious Hospitality

"Our intention creates our reality."

—Wayne Dyer

Intention is the invisible architecture behind every action, every choice, every word, every moment of presence. It is the difference between motion and meaning, between effort and alignment, between doing and *directing* your doing. Where presence brings you fully into the moment, intention gives that moment direction.

Intention is not a goal. It is not a plan. It is not an item on a to-do list or a sentence you write in January and forget by March. Intention is the energetic signature behind the actions you take. Two people can do the same thing—say the same words, follow the same process, deliver the same service—but if their intention is different, the impact is entirely different.

In hospitality, this distinction is everywhere. One team member offers a greeting because it's required. Another offers a greeting because they genuinely want the guest to feel welcome, safe, and seen. Same words. Same gesture. Completely different energy. Intention is the difference between politeness and hospitality, between meeting a standard and elevating an experience.

In leadership, intention becomes even more powerful. A leader can give feedback to correct someone—or to grow someone. They can design a process to control a team—or to empower a team. They can make decisions to protect their ego—or to protect the culture. The external action may look identical. The internal intention changes everything.

Before I understood intention, my leadership was reactive. I was moving fast, responding in real time, making decisions out of urgency, pressure, habit, or performance. I was often present in the moment, but my presence had no compass. Whatever emotion or expectation was loudest inside me became the driver. Sometimes that aligned with my values; often it did not.

Then I began to understand something simple, profound, and humbling: without intention, presence is directionless. Without presence, intention is powerless. Together, they create alignment. That realization changed how I moved through every room of my life.

Intention transforms a moment of awareness into a moment of impact. It takes your presence and channels it toward a purpose. It is how you ensure your actions aren't random, inherited, or purely reactive, but chosen. Intention is the fuel that turns consciousness into creation.

When you hold a clear, honest, grounded intention, your energy becomes a laser rather than a lantern. You stop scattering yourself across distractions. You stop leaking energy into things that don't matter. You stop reacting from ego or fear. You begin moving from clarity. And clarity is one of the greatest gifts you can offer yourself, your team, your family, and your guests. Intention is the quiet force that shapes everything you touch.

Most people confuse intention with goals. They assume they are the same — future-oriented statements about what we want to achieve. But intention lives in a completely different realm. It is not about the future at all. Intention lives in the now. It is the energy you bring to the moment you are in, not the moment you're aiming toward months from now.

A goal says, "That is where I want to go."
Intention says, "This is how I choose to show up right now."

You might reach a goal by force, pressure, comparison, fear, or sheer exhaustion. You can hit a target while being completely disconnected from yourself. Intention is different. Intention demands alignment. It demands presence. It demands honesty. It demands that your actions and your inner state are in conversation.

A goal is something you chase. Intention is something you embody.

And embodiment changes outcomes in ways goals never can. When your actions are driven purely by goals, you often slip into urgency and scarcity. You start scanning constantly for what is missing, incomplete, or behind. You push rather than align. You become efficient but not effective, productive but not purposeful, busy but not fulfilled. This is how people spend entire careers in motion but not in meaning.

Intention interrupts that cycle. It slows the system. It returns you to yourself. It shifts your focus from outcome to energy.

Earlier in this book we explored traction and distraction. Traction moves you toward alignment. Distraction pulls you away from it. Traction is not about how much you accomplish; it's about whether what you're doing is true. It's the feeling of moving in the direction your soul recognizes as right. There is a quiet ease to it—not because it lacks effort, but because it lacks inner resistance. Your inner world and outer world are finally having the same conversation.

Distraction, on the other hand, can be highly productive. That's the trap. You can be extremely busy and still deeply misaligned. You can complete tasks while ignoring your deeper truth. You can do a hundred things in a day and still feel empty at night because none of those actions were born from intention.

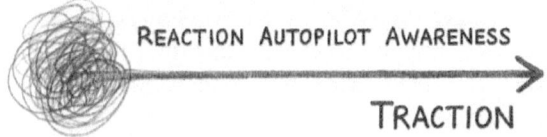

DISTRACTION

REACTION AUTOPILOT AWARENESS

TRACTION

When action has no intention, it drains you. When action is fueled by intention, it energizes you.

Intention is what makes your energy directional rather than scattered. It is the difference between walking with purpose and running without aim. It helps you distinguish urgency from importance, noise from truth, pleasing from leading, and habit from alignment. It lifts you out of the gravitational pull of distraction—the emails, alerts, demands, expectations—and brings you back into conscious choice.

Intention becomes the internal compass that guides your day. Not the inbox. Not the to-do list. Not other people's expectations. Intention works from the inside out. It sets the frequency of your day before the day touches you. It shapes your tone before you open your mouth. It directs your energy before the world has a chance to scatter it. Without intention, your energy leaks. With intention, your energy leads. And when your energy leads, life follows.

Wayne Dyer's work on intention deepened this understanding for me. In *The Power of Intention*, he describes intention not as something we *do*, but as a universal field of energy we can align with—a creative force that is always available. We don't manufacture intention; we tune into it. He speaks of the "faces" of intention—creativity, kindness, love, beauty, expansion, abundance, receptivity—as qualities of that field. When we embody those qualities, we are no longer pushing our will onto life; we are cooperating with a larger current.

That perspective shifted something fundamental in me. Intention stopped being about forcing outcomes and became about aligning with a state of being. Instead of asking, "How do I get what I want?" I began asking, "Who am I willing to be in this situation? What quality of energy do I want to bring?" Dyer often said, "You do not attract what you want; you attract what you are." Intention, then, is the daily practice of becoming the kind of person who naturally creates what they desire—not through control, but through coherence.

In practical terms, this meant moving from "I intend to hit this target" to "I intend to lead with generosity," or "I intend to bring calm and clarity," or "I intend to treat every person I meet today as if they matter." The outcomes still mattered—but they became by-products of alignment rather than measurements of worth.

Intention is not theoretical. It lives in the choices we make moment by moment, in the energy we bring to everything we do. It turns ordinary acts into sacred gestures. It transforms leadership, service, and life into something meaningful.

One of the first ways I began practicing intention daily was through morning ritual. For years, I had been waking into urgency: phone buzzing, mind racing, energy scattered before my feet even touched the floor. I was reacting to the day before it began.

I started small. Three conscious breaths before leaving the bed. Feeling my feet on the floor. A glass of water, received as nourishment rather than autopilot. A quiet question whispered inward: "How do I want to show up today? What energy do I choose to carry?" Those tiny acts created enormous ripple effects. The morning was no longer about productivity; it became about presence infused with purpose. The intention behind each action became a guidepost for the rest of the day.

At work, intention became equally transformative.

I remember leading a resort team where distractions had fractured our presence. Phones vibrated under tables during meetings. People responded reflexively rather than thoughtfully. The energy in the room felt fragmented. We were together physically, but not energetically.

Instead of lecturing about focus, I introduced a small ritual: a simple basket at the entrance of our leadership meetings. No big announcement, no judgment — just a gentle invitation. I placed my own phone there first. One by one, others followed. Almost immediately, the room felt different. People sat taller, leaned in, and listened more deeply. Laughter returned. Difficult topics became easier to navigate. The intention behind the basket was not control; it was connection. We weren't just managing distractions; we were choosing presence.

At Six Senses Ibiza, I experienced intention expressed through a guest welcome unlike anything I had seen. It wasn't staged or scripted; it was a quiet ceremony of arrival. A warm gaze. A hand placed gently on the heart. A few simple phrases offered silently or softly:

- May this be the beginning of your healing.
- May this moment bring you back to yourself.
- May this place hold you.

Guests didn't just notice the ritual; they *felt* it. Shoulders dropped. Eyes welled up. Some exhaled as if they'd been holding their breath for months. That is the power of intention: it transforms a check-in into a threshold. Space becomes sanctuary. Service becomes soul.

Intention also manifests in the micro-choices of leadership:

- The tone you choose in a tense conversation.
- The eye contact you maintain while a team member shares something vulnerable.
- The extra minute you give someone who seems off.
- The breath you take before responding to a challenging email.

Each of these choices, though small, compounds over time. They build trust. They build alignment. They build culture.

Intention isn't just a mental exercise; it is physiological. Research from the HeartMath Institute shows that when our heart rhythms, brain waves, and breath are coherent—when we intentionally align emotion with thought—our nervous system balances, our cognitive function improves, and our decision-making becomes clearer. In that state, we are not only more focused; we are also more emotionally available and less reactive. Intentional leaders don't just *do* things differently; they *radiate* differently. Their energy stabilizes the room before they speak. Their alignment becomes a kind of invisible leadership.

In terms of the Map of Consciousness, intention is the bridge that lifts us from lower frequencies driven by fear, shame, or pride into the territory of courage, willingness, and love. When you set an intention anchored in generosity, curiosity, or service, you are consciously moving your state up the scale. You are choosing the quality of energy you will transmit, and that choice has real effects on your physiology, your relationships, and your results.

As with presence and authenticity, intention cannot remain a concept if it is going to transform your life. It must be embodied. It must move from the page into your breath, your schedule, your meetings, your home. The next sections are an invitation to begin that work—to turn intention from an inspiring idea into a lived, daily practice.

PRACTICES OF INTENTION

1. The Daily Intention Pause

Before your feet touch the floor in the morning—or before stepping into any meaningful space—pause.

- Take a slow, conscious breath.
- Place a hand on your heart or your chest.
- Ask: "How do I want to show up today? What energy do I choose to bring?"

Keep the answer simple: one word or one sentence—calm, courageous, loving, curious, present. Let that be the frequency you return to throughout the day.

2. Turn Routines into Rituals

Choose one everyday activity—making coffee, arriving at your desk, beginning a team briefing, sitting down to dinner—and infuse it with intention.

- Before you begin, pause for a breath.
- Silently dedicate the action: "May this coffee ground me." "May this meeting bring clarity and connection."
- "May this meal nourish more than just our bodies."

Repetition turns ordinary routines into anchors of alignment.

3. The Alignment Check

Between tasks, especially when switching roles (leader to parent, parent to partner, partner to friend), pause for thirty seconds.

- Ask: "Am I acting from intention, or reacting from habit right now?"
- Notice your body, your tone, your pace.
- If misaligned, take one breath and consciously adjust.

This simple check prevents energy leakage and miscommunication.

4. Intentional Communication

Before a conversation—especially a difficult one—take a moment alone.

- Ask: "What do I want this person to feel at the end of this conversation?"
- Is it safe? Seen? Encouraged? Challenged with love?

Let that answer shape your words, your posture, and your pace. Feedback given with the intention to empower lands very differently from feedback given with the intention to prove you're right.

5. Environmental Anchors

Use your physical space to remind you of intention.

- A small stone on your desk you touch before calls.
- A phrase on a sticky note: "Lead with love," "Be here," "Clarity over speed."
- A basket for phones before meetings or meals.

Let your environment reflect the kind of energy you want to live in.

6. End-of-Day Coherence

Before sleep, revisit your day.

- Ask: "Where did I act with clarity and purpose today? Where did I drift into autopilot?"
- Notice without judgment.
- Offer yourself a simple intention for tomorrow: "Tomorrow, I will pause before reacting," or "Tomorrow, I will listen more than I speak."

Reflection becomes calibration rather than criticism.

7. The Intention Mirror

Before important moments—presentations, difficult conversations, family gatherings—stand in front of a mirror.

- Place a hand on your heart.
- Look into your own eyes and ask: "Am I aligned? Am I showing up in harmony with who I want to be?"
- Adjust your breath, your posture, even your facial expression until your body says yes.
- Then step into the moment from that place.

REFLECTION: LIVING WITH INTENTION

These prompts are an invitation to examine how intention currently shows up in your life and where it wants to deepen.

- Which parts of my day are most often on autopilot? Where could a simple intention transform the quality of those moments?
- What energy tends to drive my actions when I *don't* pause—urgency, fear, the need to please, the desire to prove?
- When was the last time I felt deeply aligned—as if what I was doing and who I was being were in complete harmony? What intention was present?
- Where do I notice my energy leaking—overcommitting, multitasking, saying "yes" when I mean "no?" What intention could help me reclaim that energy?
- If I could choose three words to describe the energy I want to bring into my leadership, my work, and my home, what would they be? How often am I currently living them?

- In what ways am I still treating intention as a wish for the future instead of a choice in the present?

Let your answers be honest rather than polished. Intention grows stronger each time you tell yourself the truth.

DO THE WORK: EMBODYING INTENTION

Choose one or two of these practices to work with for the next week. Let them become experiments, not obligations.

1. Daily Micro-Intention

Each morning, write a single sentence guiding your energy for the day.

- "Today, I intend to move at the speed of clarity, not urgency."
- "Today, I intend to see the person behind every role."
- "Today, I intend to listen with my whole body."

Revisit this sentence at lunchtime and before bed. Notice how it subtly shapes your choices.

2. Transition Anchors

Identify at least two transitions in your day—leaving home for work, arriving at the office, returning home, putting the kids to bed.

- For each transition, create a tiny anchor: three breaths at the door, a phrase you repeat, a moment of silence in the car before stepping out.

Use these anchors to reset your intention for the role you are about to step into.

3. Intention in Interaction

For one full day, before responding to any email, message, or request, take one conscious breath and ask: "What energy do I want to bring here?"

- Notice how this changes your tone, your timing, even your choice of medium (maybe a phone call instead of a text).
- At the end of the day, reflect: Did my interactions feel different? Did I feel more aligned?

4. Ritualize a Routine

Choose one habitual task—pouring coffee, opening your laptop, beginning a team briefing—and commit to performing it with full presence and deliberate intention for an entire week.

- Same action, new energy.
- Watch how this small ritual begins to influence not only you, but those around you.

5. The Power of Intention Journal

Inspired by Wayne Dyer's work, spend ten minutes each evening answering two questions:

- "Where today did I act as an expression of creativity, kindness, love, beauty, expansion, abundance, or receptivity?"
- "Where tomorrow would I like to embody those qualities more fully?"

Over time, you will begin to see patterns—areas of your life where intention already flows, and areas asking for more conscious care.

Intention is the heartbeat of Conscious Hospitality. It transforms service into connection, leadership into influence, and time into meaning. It is the energy behind presence, the fuel behind authenticity, and the channel through which empathy flows. When you lead with intention, everything begins to align—the room, the team, the guests, and most importantly, yourself.

As I continued to anchor intention in my life, I began to notice something remarkable: clarity of purpose alone was not enough. I could arrive with presence, act with intention, and align my energy—and still miss the mark if I did not truly feel and understand the experiences of others.

Intention sets the direction, but empathy is the vessel that carries it.

Without the ability to tune into the emotional, mental, and energetic states of the people around us, even the most well-intentioned actions can fall flat or cause unintended harm. Empathy allows presence and intention to become fully relational. It transforms alignment from a personal practice into a shared experience—a co-created field of trust, safety, and connection.

In the next chapter, we will explore empathy—not as a soft skill or a nice-to-have, but as the active, energetic capacity to perceive, feel, and respond to others with attuned care. We'll see how it became the bridge between my leadership and the teams I guided, how it shaped guest experiences that felt alive rather than scripted, and how it deepened the bonds within my own family. Empathy is what turns conscious leadership into a living, breathing force—and it is the pillar that allows every other element of Conscious Hospitality to expand, ripple, and resonate.

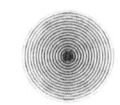

CHAPTER 8
Empathy: The Bridge to Connection

"Empathy is seeing with the eyes of another, listening with the ears of another, and feeling with the heart of another."

—Alfred Adler

It was one of those luminous afternoons on property—the kind of soft, golden light you pray for in hospitality. The lobby felt like an exhale. Guests arriving found a gentle welcome; those lingering after lunch moved slowly, soaking in the calm.

I was walking through the lobby when it happened.

A man suddenly collapsed near the entrance. His wife and two young children stood beside him, their faces instantly drained of color. In one breath, the entire frequency of the space shifted—from serenity to shock. Fear, panic, helplessness.

Our team moved quickly. Emergency protocols activated, staff calling for medical support, someone starting CPR. My role in that moment was not logistics. It was presence.

I went to the family, knelt down to the wife's eye level, and gently held her hand.

"You're not alone," I told her softly. "We're here with you. You don't have to be strong right now."

I didn't offer clichés. I didn't rush to promise that everything would be okay. I stayed with her and the children until the ambulance arrived. I kept my voice low, my breathing steady, my body grounded. I wasn't there to fix what I couldn't fix. I was there to *be* with them.

Weeks later, we reconnected. We cried. We laughed. We shared gratitude. That family still reaches out today. That day reminded me of something fundamental:

Empathy is not a reflex. Empathy is a decision.

It is the conscious choice to move toward someone's experience instead of away from it. To be with someone in their pain without erasing it. To witness without judging. To connect without correcting. In Conscious Hospitality—and in conscious leadership—that choice is what matters most.

People may not remember the system you designed or the policy you implemented. But they will never forget how you made them feel when everything fell apart. Empathy is the bridge between human experiences. It is how the soul recognizes itself in another.

Empathy is often misunderstood. It is not pity. It is not sympathy. It is not rescuing or fixing.

Pity says, "You poor thing."
Sympathy says, "I feel bad for you."
Compassion says, "I want to help you."
Empathy says, "I am here with you. I understand, even if I can't change it."

Empathy is presence in motion. It is the ability to feel *with* another human being—not to absorb their pain or carry it for them, but to sit beside it without flinching. It is meeting people where they are, not where we think they should be.

In leadership, empathy means holding space without always needing to control it. In hospitality, it means noticing what is unsaid, reading subtle cues, sensing when someone is "off" even when they insist they are fine. It means listening not only with your ears, but with your eyes, your heart, and your nervous system.

To lead with empathy, you must be willing to slow down. Presence gives you access to the moment. Authenticity lets you show up as yourself. Intention directs your energy. Empathy uses all three to connect with another person's experience.

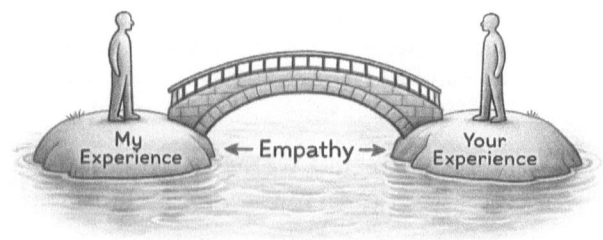

Early in my career, much of my frustration—with colleagues, teams, and even myself—came from judgment. I judged people for being slow, reactive, disengaged, too emotional, or not emotional enough. I jumped to conclusions about their motives. I wrote stories in my head and treated them as facts. I tried to correct them from a place of urgency and ego. I thought I was being decisive. In reality, I was protecting my image.

The turning point came when I began to understand that every human broadcasts a frequency—and behavior is merely the visible expression of an inner state.

I started seeing people not as problems to manage, but as stories to understand. Not as difficult, but often as dysregulated. Not as resistant, but as unseen.

Instead of asking, "What's wrong with them?" I started asking, "What might they be carrying right now?" "What part of them is trying to be heard?" "What emotion is asking for space?"

That shift—from judgment to curiosity—was transformative. It moved me out of performance and into presence, out of control and into empathy.

On the Map of Consciousness, judgment lives in the lower frequencies of anger (150) and pride (175)—tight, contracted states that create resistance and defensiveness. Curiosity, on the other hand, moves us closer to acceptance (350) and love (500)—expansive states that invite coherence, connection, and healing.

Curiosity is a form of love in motion. It allows us to meet the human experience as it is, without collapsing into it or trying to fix it, but with a sincere wish to understand and support.

In hospitality, judgment is subtle but pervasive. It sounds like:

"She's lazy," when she's actually exhausted and unsupported. "He's a difficult guest," when he's actually grieving or terrified. "They're unmotivated," when they simply haven't felt seen, valued, or safe.

One afternoon at a resort, a guest's backpack was stolen from the pool area. It wasn't just a backpack—it held her wallet, passport, and a luxury brand that carried its own emotional weight. She was furious, and understandably so. Security protocols kicked in, reports were filed, procedures followed. But what she needed first wasn't a form or an explanation; she needed someone to feel with her.

I sat with her, listened, and said, "If this had happened to me, I'd be just as upset. You are right to feel this way. Let's walk through this together." We did everything we could operationally, but the real shift came from empathy. She later told me, "What I remember most is not losing the bag. It's how you made me feel when I lost it." She became not only a loyal guest, but a friend.

That experience taught me a phrase I've carried ever since: *graciousness is luxury*. Policy can protect you. Empathy bonds you.

Curiosity allows us to listen beneath the words, see the energy beneath the behavior, and act from empathy rather than assumption. It also invites us to extend that same gentleness to ourselves—meeting our own mistakes, fears, and exhaustion with understanding instead of constant self-critique.

Because empathy that never turns inward becomes unsustainable.
People don't need you to be perfect. They need to feel safe.

Safe to speak honestly.
Safe to make mistakes.
Safe to show emotion.
Safe to be human.

Empathy is the invisible hospitality we extend first to ourselves, then to our teams, and only then to our guests. Without that safety, no one can serve with clarity, creativity, or joy. They will serve from fear, compliance, and survival—and guests will feel it, even if they cannot name it.

Our nervous systems are always listening. Every tone of voice, every micro-expression, every pause communicates either safety or threat. Polyvagal Theory, developed by Dr. Stephen Porges, describes *neuroception*—the subconscious scanning our bodies perform to determine whether we are safe or in danger. When safety is perceived, the nervous system allows curiosity, connection, and learning. When threat is sensed, we move into fight, flight, or freeze.

Empathy is the leadership skill that creates safety. It is what allows our presence, authenticity, and intention to be received.

I have seen empathy at work under extreme conditions.

In March 2020, at our hotel in Austin, COVID arrived and the world changed almost overnight. The festival we depended on—Austin City Limits—was suddenly cancelled. Bookings evaporated. Fear, confusion, and grief swept through the team. We all sensed what might be coming: layoffs, restructuring, endings.

I had to deliver news no leader wants to share. There was no way to decorate it. What mattered most in those meetings was not strategy, not a clever plan, but presence and empathy.

I gathered the team and told them the truth: "I don't have all the answers. I can't promise things I don't know. But I am here. I am listening. And we will walk through this together."

In those moments, empathy didn't remove the pain—but it held it. It softened the hardest edges of fear and created a sense of *with-ness* instead of *otherness*. We were still facing uncertainty, but we were facing it in connection. That changed everything about how we navigated the crisis.

Empathy also reshaped the way I handled performance.

There was a team member once who was consistently late, disengaged in meetings, and short with colleagues. Old me would have gone straight to correction: warnings, stricter oversight, consequences. Instead, I invited him for a walk.

"How are you *really* doing?" I asked.

He hesitated, then shared that his father was ill, he was caring for him at night, and he was terrified of losing his job on top of everything else. The behavior that looked like apathy was actually grief and exhaustion.

We adjusted his schedule, offered support, and made space for his reality. His performance improved—not because we tightened the rules, but because he finally felt safe enough to show up as he was. Empathy didn't lower the standard; it helped him rise to it.

Science has a name for this: emotional contagion. Our nervous systems sync to the most dominant energy in the room. Mirror neurons fire not just when we act, but when we observe others acting and feeling. When a leader embodies empathy—regulated, present, attuned—others unconsciously match that frequency. The room softens. Shoulders drop. People speak more honestly. They take more ownership because they feel less afraid.

Empathy, anchored in presence and intention, allows you to stand *with* others while staying rooted in your own center. This is where self-empathy becomes essential.

You cannot sustainably offer empathy to others while treating yourself with contempt. If your internal dialogue is harsh, impatient, and unforgiving, your nervous system lives in chronic defense—even if you are kind to everyone else. Over time, that dissonance fractures you.

Practicing empathy with yourself—acknowledging your limits, honoring your emotions, forgiving your missteps—is not indulgence. It is maintenance. Dr. Gabor Maté reminds us that suppressing our own truth for the sake of harmony or performance eventually shows up in the body—as tension, illness, or burnout. Self-empathy keeps the channel clear so that the empathy you extend to others is genuine, not performative.

Empathy transforms culture.

When leaders lead with empathy, feedback becomes dialogue, not condemnation. Mistakes become data, not identity. Teams move from compliance to belonging. Guests feel cared for, not processed. Families shift from walking on eggshells to walking together.

Because in the end, teams and guests alike do not respond to our titles or our strategies. They respond to our energy.

Empathy is the invisible current beneath every thriving culture. It is what makes hospitality sacred, leadership resonant, and teams alive.

And like presence, authenticity, and intention, empathy must move from concept into practice.

PRACTICES OF EMPATHY

1. Pause Before You Respond

When someone comes to you with a problem, complaint, or strong emotion, resist the urge to fix, defend, or redirect.

- Take one slow breath.
- Ask yourself silently: "What might they be feeling right now? What do they need most—solutions or support?"

Respond from that awareness rather than from your instinct to control.

2. Listen With Your Whole Body

Empathy is communicated as much through your nervous system as through your words.

- Turn your body toward the person.
- Soften your gaze.
- Drop your shoulders. Uncross your arms.
- Let your posture say: "I'm here. I'm not rushing. You matter."

Notice how often their body begins to mirror your regulation.

3. Use Empathetic Language

Replace minimizing statements ("It's not so bad," "Don't worry about it") with validating ones:

- "That sounds really hard. Thank you for telling me."
- "I can see why you'd feel that way."
- "I'm here with you. We'll walk through this together."

Language that acknowledges emotion creates space for it to move.

4. The Five-Minute Check-In

At the start of a meeting or briefing, take five minutes to check in on how people are *arriving*, not just what they are doing.

- Ask: "What's one word that describes how you're coming into today?"
- Or: "Is there anything on your heart before we dive into business?"

No analysis, no fixing—just witnessing. These small rituals build psychological safety over time.

5. Boundaries With Empathy

Empathy does not mean saying yes to everything. It means being honest and kind at the same time.

- "I care about what you're going through, and I also need to protect my own capacity. Let's see what support is possible."
- "I want to give this the attention it deserves. Can we schedule time when I can be fully present with you?"

Boundaries held with warmth deepen trust rather than erode it.

REFLECTION: HOW OPEN IS MY HEART?

Use these prompts to explore your own relationship with empathy. Let your answers be honest rather than ideal.

- When was the last time I truly felt seen, heard, or held by someone? What made that moment feel safe?
- In my leadership, do I tend to listen to *fix*, to *respond*, or to *feel*? Where could I offer more presence and less urgency?
- Who in my life might be carrying something invisible right now—at work or at home? What small act of curiosity or care could I offer them?
- How do I usually respond to strong emotion—my own or others'? Do I shut down, speed up, change the subject, give advice? What would softening look like instead?
- Where do I need to extend empathy to myself—around exhaustion, disappointment, or fear? What would it sound like to speak to myself the way I speak to someone I love?
- How might my leadership or parenting change if I assumed, by default, that everyone I meet is carrying something I cannot see?

Remember: the more gently you meet your own experience, the more naturally you will meet others.

DO THE WORK: STRENGTHENING EMPATHY

Choose one or two practices to work with over the next week. Let them be experiments in energy, not exercises in perfection.

1. The Empathy Walk

Choose one person you interact with regularly—a team member, colleague, or family member.

- Spend five minutes imagining a day in their life. Their commute. Their worries. Their invisible load.
- Then send a small act of acknowledgment: a text, a question, a thank you, a moment of undivided attention.

Notice how your perception of them—and their response to you—shift.

2. Three Levels of Listening

During conversations, observe yourself.

- Level 1: Listening to respond (preparing your answer).
- Level 2: Listening to understand (focusing on their words).
- Level 3: Listening to feel (attuning to emotion, tone, and energy).

Practice moving deliberately from Level 1 to Level 3 at least once per day.

3. Empathetic Journaling

At the end of the day, write down:

- One moment you chose empathy.
- One moment you reacted from judgment or impatience.
- How you might respond differently next time.

This reflection rewires your nervous system for more attuned choices in the future.

4. Rewrite a Reactive Moment

Bring to mind a recent interaction where you felt reactive—annoyed with a guest, frustrated with a colleague, short with your child.

- On paper, rewrite the scene as if you had paused, breathed, and responded from empathy.
- What would you have said? How would your body have been different?

Imagining a new script creates new neural pathways your system can use next time.

5. Create an Empathy Ritual With Your Team

Introduce a simple ritual into your team culture:

- A one-word emotional check-in at the start of shifts.
- A practice of asking, "Is now a good time?" before giving feedback.
- A weekly moment where everyone shares one appreciation for a colleague.

These rituals teach people, over time, that how they *are* matters as much as what they *do*.

Empathy is not a performance—it is a presence. Practiced consistently, it transforms culture, relationships, and leadership. It is the bridge that carries presence, authenticity, and intention into every human interaction.

As we move toward the final pillar of the Conscious Hospitality Framework, it becomes clear that none of these elements—presence, authenticity, intention, empathy—stand alone. They are interconnected frequencies, each amplifying the others. To fully realize their power, we must learn how to weave them together in the rhythms of daily life.

That is the work of integration.

In the next chapter, we will explore how these principles move from isolated practices into a unified way of being—how they shape our decisions, our teams, our families, and the cultures we create. Integration is where Conscious Hospitality stops being a framework on the page and becomes a living, breathing expression of who you are in the world.

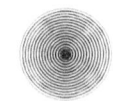

CHAPTER 9
Integration: Bridging the Gap

"Wholeness is not achieved by cutting off a portion of one's being, but by integration of the contraries."

—Carl Jung

We were sitting under the olive trees late into the evening, long after the rest of the world had surrendered to silence. The stars were sharp. The wine was deep. And as often happens when I am with people who know me beyond the roles I play, I found myself searching out loud—speaking about everything I had been learning. The books I had devoured, the insights that had reshaped me, the realizations I had carried like precious stones in my pocket. My words poured out quickly, in that familiar mix of excitement and urgency that comes when the mind has raced far ahead of the body.

My friend listened quietly, patiently, without interrupting. When I finally paused, he took a slow breath, looked at me with a depth that only comes from lived experience, and said gently, "David, you don't need more. You need to live what you already know."

It landed like a soft thunder. Not loud. Not dramatic. But undeniable.

In that moment, I realized I had crossed a threshold that many of us reach without recognizing it. I was full of wisdom but thin in practice—rich in insight, poor in embodiment. I could speak beautifully about presence, but in truth, I was still moving far too fast. I understood intention, yet distraction easily hijacked my attention. I valued empathy, but I didn't always offer it to myself. I carried authenticity like a banner, yet often drifted into performance when fear or conditioning crept in.

I had knowledge, but I had not become the knowledge. I had collected truths but had not yet lived them.

This is the hidden gap that so many leaders, seekers, and humans unknowingly inhabit—the space between *understanding* and *embodying*. We mistake accumulation for integration, depth of insight for depth of change. We read, listen, learn, and awaken intellectually, but we do not always allow these insights to transform the way we breathe, speak, lead, love, and show up in the quiet corners of life.

That night under the olive trees was the moment I understood something profound: transformation is not about learning more—it is about remembering to be more.

Integration is where ideas become identity. Where concepts become character. Where wisdom becomes your way of walking in the world.

It called me out of theory and into practice, out of performing and into living, out of aspiration and into alignment. That moment was the beginning of my true integration, and it is the essence of this chapter. Because Conscious Hospitality is not an intellectual framework. It is a way of being. It only becomes real when it moves from your mind into your nervous system, from your values into your voice, from your intentions into your actions. Integration is the moment it all becomes you.

Integration is not a step in the process. It is the transformation itself. It is the moment when your inner world—your beliefs, values, and intentions—aligns with your outer world—your choices, tone, presence, and behavior. It is when presence stops being something you practice and becomes the way you inhabit your life. When authenticity stops being an aspiration and becomes the way you speak. When intention stops being a ritual and becomes the quiet current directing your day. When empathy stops being something you extend and becomes the natural lens through which you see others.

Integration is the end of fragmentation. The end of compartmentalized living. The end of saying one thing and embodying another. It is the return to coherence.

Because we all know the tension of living out of alignment. Saying yes when our body whispers no. Speaking about balance while rushing through our days. Teaching empathy while being hard on ourselves. Promising presence while checking our phones during dinner. These moments do not make us hypocrites—they make us human. But they also illuminate something deeper: the ache of dis-integration.

Disintegration happens when our values live in our mind but not yet in our habits, when our truth stays trapped in reflection but not fully expressed in action. It is not moral failure—it is energetic friction. It is the quiet drain that comes from knowing who we could be and sensing the distance between that possibility and our behavior. This friction doesn't just impact others. It impacts us. It erodes self-trust, dims our intuition, and leaves us exhausted in ways we struggle to articulate.

We feel the gap. And so does everyone around us.

Guests may not know your mission statement, but they feel whether it is being lived. Teams may not articulate misalignment, but they sense when the leader's energy contradicts their words. Children may not understand the nuance, but they feel the difference between true presence and half-attention.

This is why integration matters. Because leadership is energetic before it is operational. Parenting is energetic before it is instructional. Hospitality is energetic before it is procedural. Integration is coherence in motion.

And coherence is the true engine of influence.

But integration does not ask for perfection. It asks for return. It asks for the willingness to realign—again and again—each time we drift. It is not about being flawless. It is about being faithful. Over time, these returns accumulate. Values become habits. Habits become patterns. Patterns become identity. And identity becomes impact.

Integration is not loud. It does not announce itself. It shows up quietly in the way you breathe before speaking, the way you listen without rushing, the way you welcome emotions without trying to fix them, the way you transition from work to home with full presence instead of carrying remnants of the day into your living room. It shows up in the softening of your tone, the quality of your gaze, the steadiness of your nervous system, the trust others feel in your presence.

Integration is not about becoming someone new. It is about becoming someone true.

To integrate consciously is to bring the same values to every arena of your life—work, home, and the inner world—not as compartments but as reflections of one coherent self. Integration is the harmony of the three worlds we inhabit daily.

At work, integration asks you to bring presence into meetings, authenticity into conversations, intention into planning, and empathy into feedback. It asks you to lead from wholeness rather than performance. It turns your leadership from managerial into magnetic.

At home, integration asks you to bring the same quality of presence you offer guests to your children, the same empathy you extend to colleagues to your partner, the same intention you bring to strategy to your rituals of connection. It transforms the household not through perfection but through attentiveness, repair, and genuine availability.

In yourself, integration becomes the quiet work of telling the truth about your thoughts and emotions, choosing values over habits, grounding your nervous system before reacting, and treating yourself with the same empathy you offer others. Integration begins within. Without inner coherence, outer coherence is impossible.

Leadership is not built in public moments. It is built in these private returns to alignment.

I learned this unexpectedly one evening at home. I had just spent hours teaching presence to executives, speaking about conscious leadership, coherence, and awareness. But when I walked in the door, I slipped immediately into distraction—phone in hand, mind racing while my son tried to share a story. He stopped mid-sentence, looked at me, and said, "Papa, are you even listening?" The sting was deep—and deserved.

I realized then that integration is measured not by what we teach, but by how we live when no one is watching.

I apologized. I put the phone away. I sat down with him, looked him in the eyes, and said, "You're right. I'm here now." It was a small moment, but it was a moment of integration—the alignment of principle and presence.

I experienced something similar in a high-stakes situation at one resort. A difficult guest incident had shaken the team. The instinct might have been to jump immediately into analysis, solutions, or process correction. Instead, I gathered the team and created space for the emotional landscape first— naming what happened, acknowledging how it felt, breathing together, giving presence before performance. Only after everyone had grounded could we talk about solutions. That moment wasn't about strategy. It was about coherence. Empathy paved the way for clarity.

Integration is never about grand gestures. It is about consistency—the quiet, repeated choices that align behavior with truth. Over time, these choices create a gravitational pull around your leadership. People feel safer. They open up more. They trust more deeply. They follow not because they have to, but because your presence invites coherence in them, too.

Integration is not a destination you arrive at once. It is a rhythm you live inside—a continual choosing of alignment over performance, coherence over urgency, purpose over habit.

And like all transformations, integration deepens through practice.

Before we move forward into the next part of the book, the moment has come for you to step into your own integration—not as a concept, but as a lived experience.

LET'S PRACTICE: BRINGING IT ALL TO LIFE—ONE HABIT AT A TIME

Integration happens through small, grounded, repeatable practices that build coherence over time. These are not about perfection. They are about returning to alignment again and again.

1. Create a Daily Integration Ritual

At the start or end of each day, ask yourself:

- Did I act in alignment with who I say I want to be?
- Where was I present? Where was I distracted?
- Did I lead with intention or simply react?
- Was I honest with myself and others?
- Did I practice empathy in the way I spoke, listened, or moved through my day?

Reflect, write, or simply sit with the answers. Awareness is the seed of integration.

2. Design Your Week from the Blueprint

Before the week begins, look at your calendar and consider:

- Where do I need to be fully present?
- Where might I drift into performance instead of authenticity?
- What am I doing out of habit rather than intention?
- Who might need empathy, understanding, or grounding from me this week?

Let your values shape your schedule—not the other way around.

3. Use Transitions as Integration Moments

Life unfolds in transitions. Build micro-rituals:

- Three breaths before entering your home.
- A grounding pause before leading a meeting.
- A moment of release after a difficult conversation.

These small shifts recalibrate your energy and bring coherence to each role you step into.

4. Create a Weekly Alignment Check-In with Your Team or Family

Choose a time to ask:

- What went well this week?
- Where did we live our values?
- Where did we drift?
- What intention do we want to hold for the week ahead?

This rhythm builds collective coherence and shared responsibility for alignment.

5. Choose One Principle to Embody Each Week

Don't integrate everything at once. Rotate weekly:

- Practice Presence
- Embody Authenticity
- Move with Intention
- Lead with Empathy

Depth over breadth creates real change.

REFLECTION: WHERE AM I LIVING WHAT I KNOW?

This reflection is not for judgment—it is for honesty.

- Where in my life am I most aligned?
- Where am I most fragmented?
- What is the cost of that fragmentation?
- Which principle feels strongest in me right now—and why?
- Which principle am I resisting—and what might that resistance be teaching me?
- What would a fully integrated version of me feel like in this season of my life?

DO THE WORK:
PRACTICES TO EMBODY YOUR VALUES IN REAL TIME

1. The Weekly Integration Scan

Take fifteen minutes weekly to ask:

- What energized me?
- What drained me?
- Where did I live the Blueprint well?
- Where did I drift from alignment?
- What is my focus for this week?
- What support do I need?

2. Build Your Personal Integration Map

- Map three circles: Work, Home, Self.
- Write aligned actions in each.
- The overlap is your integration zone—your true north.

3. Create an "Integrity Trigger"

Choose a subtle cue—a bracelet, a word, a background—to gently call you back to alignment when you drift.

4. Schedule Sacred Space

Block monthly time for solitude to reflect, recalibrate, and return to what matters most.

5. Turn Your Blueprint Into a Living Document

- Write a short commitment for each principle.
- Review it each morning.
- Let it evolve with you.

Integration is not the end of the Conscious Hospitality framework—it is the beginning of its embodied expression. It is the bridge between knowing and living, between concept and character, between the leader you have been and the leader you are becoming. Because when who you are matches how you lead, everything changes: trust deepens, influence expands, teams rise, families soften, and the spaces you inhabit begin to feel different. More grounded. More human. More real.

And real is what people remember.

Now that the framework has become alive within you, we can turn toward the spaces where it matters most—beginning with the workplace. In the next chapter, we explore how Conscious Hospitality reshapes team dynamics, nervous systems, communication patterns, and cultures, turning organizations into environments where coherence and human connection become the true markers of excellence.

This is where the work begins—where you step out of theory and into the living, breathing world of conscious leadership in action.

PART III
APPLYING CONSCIOUS HOSPITALITY

CHAPTER 10
Conscious Hospitality at Work

"Culture eats strategy for breakfast."

—Peter Drucker

There is a moment every leader knows, though most never speak about it. A moment when you walk into a room and, before anyone has said a word, you already know everything. The energy tells you. The way people are sitting, or not sitting. The silence, or the tension behind the chatter. The speed at which people move. The quality of their breathing. The look in their eyes. It is a snapshot of a team's nervous system, and it is more accurate than any KPI or dashboard. It reveals what's happening beneath the work—beneath the checklists, beneath the SOPs, beneath the polished exterior. It tells you the truth. And in hospitality, the truth is always energetic before it becomes operational.

I learned this early in my career, long before I had the language to describe it. Long before I understood concepts like coherence, emotional contagion, or the Map of Consciousness. Long before neuroscience confirmed what the best hotel GMs have known intuitively for decades: that people don't just work in environments—they tune to them. They attune, emotionally and physiologically, to the person who has the strongest frequency in the room. Leadership becomes less about title and more about nervous-system regulation. It's not metaphorical; it's biological.

Across twenty years and eleven different destinations, I saw this play out again and again. In Hawaii, where the pace of life encourages a natural spaciousness, the team's energy rose and fell with the seasons—the summer rush bringing excitement and exhaustion, the quieter months restoring presence. In Hong Kong, where intensity is embedded into the city's heartbeat, the team moved fast and felt fast. People spoke quickly, walked quickly, reacted quickly. I had to adjust the pace of my own energy to help slow them down when necessary and accelerate with purpose when it mattered. In Mexico, where warmth is woven into culture, the team taught me what it means to feel held by your

95

colleagues—not through words, but through small gestures that communicate, "I have you." In Ibiza, the teams carried a different kind of frequency—creative, expressive, spiritually curious. They wanted not only to do great work but to understand why it mattered.

And then there were teams that looked flawless on paper but were silently collapsing. Teams performing with technical excellence but emotional emptiness. Teams that smiled at guests and disconnected from each other. Teams with impeccable standards and no sense of belonging. Those were the moments when I understood the real difference between a brand and a culture. A brand is what you tell the world. A culture is what the world feels when they encounter your people.

I remember arriving at a property—beautiful, polished, immaculate—where everything "worked." Service scores were solid. Financials were healthy. Guests were satisfied. But something was missing. I could feel it the moment I walked through the employee entrance. The air was heavy, shoulders were tight, smiles were polite but not alive. People moved efficiently, but not joyfully. There was no warmth in the break room, no spark in morning lineups, no laughter. Hospitality was happening, technically—but not energetically. And guests, whether consciously or not, always feel the difference.

I didn't start with strategy. I started with people. I asked simple questions that leaders often avoid because they require courage, honesty, and vulnerability:

"How does it feel to arrive at work each day?"
"What part of your day drains you?"
"What gives you meaning here?"
"When was the last time you laughed with a colleague?"
"When did you last feel genuinely appreciated?"

The answers were raw:

"I don't feel seen."
"I'm afraid of making mistakes."
"I'm overwhelmed."
"No one asks how we are."
"It feels transactional."
"I miss connection."

Not one person asked for a better SOP.
Not one person asked for a new benefit.
Not one person asked for higher standards.

They asked for humanity.
So we made humanity the strategy.

We created simple rituals—not grand initiatives, not expensive programs, not complex structures. Just small, human, intentional practices. Morning grounding breaths. Two-minute presence resets before the busiest shifts. A Friday gratitude circle. Storytelling moments where someone shared a guest interaction that moved them or a lesson learned during the week. Leaders walking the employee entrance with genuine warmth, not managerial posture. Small, heartfelt acknowledgments that weren't tied to performance metrics but to effort, courage, kindness, and character.

It took less than three weeks to feel the shift. Energy rose. Conversations deepened. People smiled from their eyes, not their lips. Guests noticed a calmness, a groundedness, a warmth. We didn't "fix" operations—we restored coherence. And coherence always improves performance. Always.

This is why I believe—to my core—that the true work of leadership is energetic, not just functional. A leader is not simply a manager of tasks but a regulator of emotional climate. Your nervous system becomes the thermostat for the entire team. If you walk in anxious, everyone tightens subconsciously. If you walk in grounded, everyone breathes deeper. If you walk in distracted, people lose direction. If you walk in with intent, people rise.

Neuroscientists call this emotional contagion. Polyvagal Theory calls it neuroception—the subconscious detection of safety or danger. David Hawkins calls it calibration. I simply call it leadership. You can feel the nervous system of a team the same way you can feel the temperature of a room. And the leader's frequency determines that temperature long before a word is spoken.

I remember a morning in Austin when everything that could go wrong did. Last-minute cancellations, staffing shortages, guest complaints, operational fires. It was chaos. My instinct was to match the pace of everything happening around me—but I caught myself. If I walked into that briefing carrying anxiety, I'd ignite the whole team's fight-or-flight response. So instead, I paused in the corridor outside the meeting room. Three breaths. Shoulders down. Back straight. I entered slowly, intentionally, looking people in the eyes. "Good morning, everyone. Let's take one breath together before we begin." The room shifted instantly. Not because I had the answers—but because I had the energy.

During COVID, this understanding became even more essential. I had to look team members in the eyes and tell them hard truths: furloughs, uncertainty, cuts, closures. There is no training manual for that moment. There is only presence. I told them what I knew. I told them what I didn't know. I told them I was here, with them, in this storm. I didn't offer false hope. I offered connection. It didn't remove the fear—but it gave fear a place to rest. Months later, many told me, "That moment changed how I saw leadership." Not because of what I said, but because of how I said it. Calm is not passive. Calm is powerful. Calm regulates. Calm stabilizes. Calm leads.

Another time, in Mexico, I witnessed one of the strongest team cultures I have ever seen—not because people were perfect, but because they were united. They celebrated each other. They anticipated each other's needs. They insisted on excellence but never weaponized it. When someone was struggling, someone else quietly stepped in. When someone succeeded, everyone cheered. There was no competition, only contribution. That team worked less like a department and more like a choir: each voice distinct, each one indispensable, each one attuning to the others. They were in harmony.

I've also led teams where people were technically outstanding but emotionally disconnected. Teams where people were afraid to speak. Teams where conflict simmered beneath polite silence. Teams where leaders performed leadership instead of practicing it. In those environments, the guest experience always suffered—not immediately, but inevitably. Hospitality is a relational art. If the relationships behind the scenes are misaligned, the experience in front of guests will always carry the weight of that misalignment.

Sometimes misalignment is subtle. It shows up in the way people avoid eye contact. In the way they walk quickly past each other. In the way voices tighten. In the way laughter disappears. In the way meetings become transactional. In the way feedback becomes a shield. In the way people stop asking questions. In the way creativity dries up. None of these seem dramatic on their own—but together, they reveal a culture losing oxygen.

I remember asking a leadership team once, "What does it feel like to walk through your employee entrance?" Not one person could answer confidently. That was the moment I knew the issue wasn't operational—it was emotional. The back-of-house is always the truest reflection of leadership. You can polish the lobby, elevate the suites, refine the restaurant, perfect the amenities—but if the heart of the house is depleted, disconnected, or fearful, hospitality becomes a performance instead of a transmission.

One of the most important insights I've learned from David Hawkins' work is that human beings operate at different energetic states—different frequencies—depending on their emotional condition. Shame (20), guilt (30), fear (100), anger (150), pride (175) are contracting states. Courage (200), willingness (310), acceptance (350), love (500) are expanding states. If a team is operating in fear, pressure, or resentment, their actions may look the same, but their impact will not. Lower frequencies create resistance. Higher frequencies create flow.

A room attendant in shame will clean a room quickly but without connection. A server in fear will deliver a tray flawlessly but without presence. A manager in pride will enforce standards but cannot elevate culture. The emotional state becomes the quality of the work.

This is why Conscious Hospitality isn't theoretical. It's physiological. It is the art of leading human beings into coherence—where their emotional states align with higher frequencies, and their work becomes a natural extension of their inner state.

One moment I will never forget was when I found a room attendant crying quietly near the service elevator at one of our resorts. She had made a mistake earlier in the day and was convinced she would be reprimanded. Her energy had collapsed into shame. Instead of correcting her, I sat on the floor next to her. I listened. I helped her breathe. I normalized the mistake and helped her reinterpret the story she was telling herself. Over time, her energy shifted upward. Months later she was leading new hires. Not because of technical training, but because someone helped her regulate an emotional state.

Leadership is often about these micro-moments—the small interactions that shape the nervous system of a team. They are not grand gestures, but accumulated signals of safety. When people feel safe, they innovate. When they feel safe, they contribute. When they feel safe, they take risks. Safety is the soil in which high-performance grows.

I've seen the same principle apply in conflict resolution. When a guest escalated from frustration to anger at a resort during a fully booked weekend, I stepped in. I didn't match their tone. I didn't defend the property. I didn't rush. I breathed. I acknowledged their frustration with sincerity. Slowly, their energy shifted—from anger to pride to courage. Within minutes, we found a solution. Not because of policy, but because of presence.

This is what happens when a leader influences a frequency field instead of trying to control a situation. You guide energy upward. You create coherence. You regulate the room. You lead without forcing.

This is why I believe influence can be expressed as a simple equation:

Influence = Frequency × Resonance.

Frequency is how consistently you show up aligned.
Resonance is the emotional tone people feel from you.

When both are high, the entire team rises.

One leader in coherence can shift the energy of thirty people.
One leader in fear can collapse the energy of thirty people.

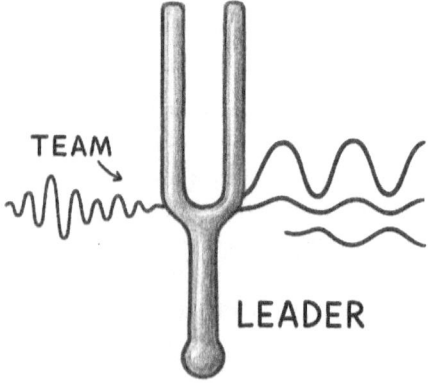

Teams follow energy, not authority.

And culture—real culture, the kind that people remember—is built in every micro-interaction, every breath before a meeting, every pause before responding, every moment you choose to regulate instead of react, every time you choose humanity over hierarchy.

This is Conscious Hospitality at work: leadership as energetic stewardship; culture as emotional coherence; teams as living systems that respond to presence, intention, authenticity, and empathy long before they respond to instructions.

And if you want to create a high-performing team, you don't start with the guests—you start with the people who take care of the guests. You start by making the invisible visible. You start by remembering that behind every role, every uniform, every task, there is a human nervous system wanting to feel safe, valued, seen, and connected.

PRACTICES OF CONSCIOUS HOSPITALITY AT WORK

A powerful way to bring Conscious Hospitality into the workplace is to translate awareness into action through simple, repeatable rituals. One of the most effective practices is conducting a weekly energy scan—not as a formal meeting, but as a quiet observation of the emotional climate. Without judgment, you walk through the property and tune into how people seem to be feeling. Are they rushed? Tense? Playful? Engaged? Scattered? Does the energy flow easily between teams, or does it feel blocked? By attuning to the team's emotional landscape, you learn where presence, support, or recalibration is needed before problems become visible.

Another transformative practice is introducing micro-rituals—small anchors that regulate the nervous system of the team. This might look like beginning meetings with a shared breath, closing the week with a gratitude moment, or placing phones aside during leadership gatherings to signal full presence. These small rituals communicate something profound: we value coherence, connection, and attention. Over time, they become part of the team's rhythm, shaping a culture where people feel held and aligned.

A third practice is the integrity check: a self-reflection moment before high-stakes interactions. Before delivering feedback, solving a problem, or walking into a tense room, you pause and ask yourself—not intellectually but somatically—"What energy am I bringing in?" This small moment of self-regulation can prevent miscommunication, de-escalate conflict, and align your actions with the culture you want to build.

REFLECTION: EXPLORING YOUR LEADERSHIP FIELD

Reflection is where the internal landscape of leadership becomes clear. Take ten minutes and explore where your presence is creating coherence and where it may be creating contraction. Ask yourself: *Where is my team's energy most aligned? Which individuals or departments carry heaviness, tension, or anxiety? How does my own emotional state influence the people around me— even when I don't intend it?* Consider recent moments of pressure or conflict. Did your presence anchor the room or agitate it? Reflect on the subtle rituals your team already has—spoken or unspoken. Are these rituals strengthening connection, or reinforcing disconnection?

These reflections reveal not just where the team stands but where you stand as the emotional center of that team. They help you become a conscious architect of the culture you want—one breath, one conversation, one moment at a time.

DO THE WORK: EMBODYING CONSCIOUS TEAM LEADERSHIP

To bring this chapter into lived experience, choose one or two practices and commit to them for the next month. Begin with a weekly integration scan—fifteen minutes of honest observation where you note what energized the team, what drained them, what moments sparked connection, and what moments diminished it. Over time, you will begin to see patterns that allow you to intervene with intention instead of reaction.

Create a living Team Blueprint: a simple document where you note the rituals, energy patterns, interventions, and cultural signals that matter most. Update it weekly. Share insights with your leadership team. Let it evolve as the team evolves. This becomes your map—a guide to leading a team not through pressure but through presence.

Finally, practice transitional micro-resets throughout the day. Two or three times daily, pause for a breath before entering a new space, a new conversation, or a new energy field. This is how leaders regulate themselves so they can regulate teams. This is how you move from managing tasks to shaping culture.

When you commit to these practices consistently, Conscious Hospitality becomes more than a concept. It becomes the living field through which your team operates. It becomes a culture your people feel, guests sense, and the world remembers.

As powerful as Conscious Hospitality is in the workplace, its true depth emerges when these principles follow you home. Leadership is not something you turn on and off with a uniform or a badge. Your presence, your energy, your alignment—they travel with you. And home is often where the truest tests of your coherence appear. In the next chapter, we explore how Conscious Hospitality becomes the foundation of family life—where leadership meets love, where presence becomes intimacy, and where empathy becomes the heartbeat of connection.

CHAPTER 11
Conscious Hospitality at Home

"Children are not things to be molded, but people to be unfolded."

—Jess Lair

Home is the one place where every mask falls off. No guest scores, no leadership presentations, no titles or accolades, no Five-Star standards to meet—just the truth of who we are when the door closes and no one is watching. I've spent more than two decades leading teams across continents, solving crises, elevating service, and navigating cultures. Yet none of it taught me more about conscious leadership than the four walls I returned to every night. Nothing humbled me more. Nothing revealed my blind spots more quickly. Nothing stretched my heart wider. And nothing grounded me more deeply than learning, slowly and sometimes painfully, how to bring the principles of Conscious Hospitality into the place that mattered most: my own home.

For years, my leadership identity and my household identity existed in two separate worlds. At work, I was composed, thoughtful, intentional. At home, I often defaulted into old patterns—reactivity, urgency, distraction, performance. It wasn't intentional; it was conditioning. The emotional habits from my childhood, the scarcity patterns, the people-pleasing tendencies, the survival reflexes—they didn't show up in the boardroom. They showed up during bedtime routines, during difficult conversations, during moments when my children were vulnerable, during disagreements with Jessica, during the small, ordinary rituals that make up family life.

The truth is this: home is the truest test of consciousness. Work gives us structure. Home gives us mirrors. And if we're willing to look, really look, home becomes the most transformative leadership training of all.

I realized this slowly, over years of stumbling through moments where my intentions were good but my presence was split. I'd walk into the house after a long day, physically present but mentally still in the afterglow of a good meeting or the residue of a stressful decision. One day, Andrés—still small at the time—ran up to me, eyes bright, excited to share something he had built. I responded with a distracted "That's great, buddy," while scrolling through an email. He went quiet. The light dimmed. And then the question I'll never forget: "Papa, did you even see it?" He wasn't asking about the toy. He was asking about himself.

It wasn't the first time I had missed a moment, but it was the first time I realized the cost. Not the cost to him—he bounced back quickly—but the cost to the relationship, to trust, to the feeling of mattering. At work, my presence was a gift; at home, it was a responsibility. And for years, I had been giving the best of my presence to everyone except the people who needed it most.

The shift didn't happen overnight. It began with humility—recognizing that leadership at home is not a continuation of leadership at work. It is a different language entirely. A different frequency. A different type of attunement. And in my house, someone was already fluently speaking that language long before I understood its grammar.

Jessica.

I've said this often: she is the emotional center of our home. But it took me years to understand what that really meant. She leads in ways that are unspoken but unmistakable. She perceives what I miss. She feels beneath the surface. She knows the temperature of our home before anyone else does. I used to think I had two jobs—one at work, one at home. But I didn't. I had one job at work. And at home, I had a place. And that place was not always the leader.

The night she told me, half joking but fully truthful, "You're the GM of the hotel, but I'm the CEO of this household," I laughed. Then I sat with it. And slowly, it landed in my body like a bell. It wasn't a power statement. It wasn't a challenge. It was a reality check—one that freed me from the unconscious weight of trying to lead where I wasn't meant to lead. Learning my place in the household wasn't about hierarchy—it was about attunement. It taught me how to support without controlling, how to show up without dominating, how to lead in partnership instead of performance.

In hospitality, we learn the subtle art of reading a room. At home, Jessica taught me to read a family. To understand how energy flows through small bodies and big emotions. How children don't react to what you say—they react to the nervous system behind your words. How the way you close a door matters just as much as what you say behind it. How a child's outburst is often a plea for connection, not correction. How a partner's silence can be an invitation to slow down, not speed up.

These were lessons no leadership academy ever taught me. They came through lived moments—many beautiful, many messy. Moments like the time Luna had a meltdown before school, overwhelmed by something that made sense only to her six-year-old heart. My instinct was to fix it, to move quickly, to regain control of the morning rhythm. Jessica stepped in gently, knelt beside her, and whispered something I couldn't hear. Within seconds, Luna softened, leaned into her, and exhaled. It wasn't what Jessica said. It was how she said it. It was the frequency behind it. The coherence. The emotional safety. Watching them, I realized that I wasn't witnessing parenting—I was witnessing energy work.

This was conscious hospitality in its purest form: attunement, presence, grace.

And then there were the moments that stretched me. The nights when Andrés came home from a long day at school carrying emotions he didn't yet know how to articulate. Or the evenings when Cruz needed time, not solutions. When Luna's sensitivity was not a trait to "manage," but a gift to honor. When my instinct to speak needed to be replaced with an instinct to listen. When old patterns emerged in me—reactivity, impatience, urgency—and I had to pause, breathe, recalibrate, and choose a different response.

Children, I learned, are master teachers. Not because they know more, but because they feel more. They feel energy long before language. They feel authenticity long before analysis. They feel presence long before they understand what presence means. They know when you're there. And they know when you're not.

There was a night when Andrés was upset about something that seemed small to me. I immediately went into problem-solving mode—explaining, rationalizing, offering solutions. He listened politely, then said, "Papa, I don't need advice. I need you to listen." There it was—simple, direct, wise. In that moment, my twelve-year-old son became my teacher. And I realized once again that conscious leadership is not about leading others; it's about being awake enough to understand when life is leading you.

I've learned to apologize more at home than I ever have in my professional life. Not because I make more mistakes—but because the impact of those mistakes is deeper. When I apologize to my children, something shifts in me. It disarms the ego. It quiets the impulse to be right. It strengthens the bond. And it teaches them that leadership is not perfection—it's accountability.

And then there is my relationship with my own parents, especially my mother. For many years, our relationship was layered with pain, misunderstanding, and emotional residue from an upbringing that shaped me in ways I am still discovering. Forgiveness was not a single decision—it was a long, slow unraveling of expectations, wounds, and inherited patterns. Conscious hospitality softened the edges of that relationship too. It allowed me to speak to her with presence instead of defensiveness, to understand the context of her life, to listen beneath her words, and to reconnect from a place of compassion rather than judgment. It wasn't instant. It wasn't perfect. But it was healing.

This is the essence of conscious hospitality at home: the willingness to see people—not as their behavior, not as their roles, not as their past—but as human beings doing the best they can with the emotional tools they inherited and the awareness they currently have. It is presence in motion. It is empathy in action. It is intention expressed through small, sacred gestures. It is authenticity lived in the rawness of family life.

And none of it works without presence. Everything we explored in Chapter 6 becomes ten times more real at home. Your phone is the enemy of connection. Your divided attention is the quickest way to erode trust. Your silence carries meaning. Your sigh carries meaning. Your body language carries meaning. Everything is information. Everything is felt.

And yet, when you get it right—when you breathe before reacting, when you look your child in the eyes, when you slow down enough to truly listen, when you allow your partner's instincts to guide the emotional rhythm—you create a home where people feel safe to be themselves. A home where nervous systems regulate instead of collapse. A home where connection becomes the anchor. A home where love is not an abstraction but an energy.

As I deepened my understanding of presence at home, I began seeing patterns that had been invisible to me for years. I noticed how quickly I could shift from openness to tension without realizing it. How I could be calm at work yet impatient at home. How the emotional residue from a long day could follow me through the front door like a subtle shadow. I began to understand that my leadership at home wasn't determined by what I said—but by the state of my nervous system when I said it.

This is why Conscious Hospitality at home is not just emotional; it's physiological. Children are master interpreters of nervous system energy. They feel dysregulation in a second. They sense irritation even when you "say the right thing." They feel when you're distracted even when you're physically near them. They feel energetic distance. They feel emotional shutdown. They feel the tension you haven't named.

But they also feel coherence. They feel presence. They feel when you're settled, when you're listening, when you're open. They feel the difference between a parent who is operating from stress and a parent who is operating from love.

The nervous system became one of my greatest teachers. I noticed that the more coherent, regulated, and grounded I was, the more naturally my children opened up to me. The more my presence softened, the more their energy softened. The calmer my breath became, the more conflict dissipated without effort. The more I practiced remaining centered, the more trust was built quietly, invisibly, steadily, day after day.

This wasn't about being calm all the time. It was about noticing when I wasn't—and making small, conscious shifts. Sometimes it was three deep breaths before responding. Sometimes it was sitting down on the floor at their level. Sometimes it was turning off the phone, even mid-sentence. Sometimes it was simply saying, "Give me one minute to regulate so I can respond from the right place."

One day, while dealing with a stressful situation at SHA, I got home still buzzing with adrenaline. Cruz came to ask me something and my tone came out sharper than intended. He immediately recoiled. That moment hurt. It took only a single sentence from me, delivered with the wrong energy, to show me how quickly my state affected him. I took a breath, knelt down, and apologized: "That wasn't fair. I'm carrying something from work, and it had nothing to do with you. I'm sorry." He softened instantly. Not because I was perfect, but because I was human—and willing to repair.

Repairing, I've learned, is one of the most powerful forms of leadership at home. Not perfection. Not solving. Repair. Being willing to come back, reconnect, realign. Being willing to show your children and your partner that love isn't fragile—it's resilient. Repair creates safety. And safety creates connection.

This is something Jessica has always understood intuitively. She doesn't get caught in needing to be right. She focuses on being connected. She doesn't rush to win arguments. She seeks to understand. Her leadership at home is rooted in emotional maturity, not control. It is grounded in intuition, attunement, and something I can only describe as heart-centered wisdom. Watching her over the years has been like watching a masterclass in conscious leadership—one without slides, without theory, without terminology. Just presence. Just awareness. Just love in motion.

Learning my place in the household meant learning how to support that wisdom—not compete with it. It meant understanding that leadership roles shift depending on context. It meant embracing the truth that while I may be the general manager in my professional life, I am not always the leader at home. And that is not a demotion—it is a blessing. A relief. A realignment of how leadership actually works in a family.

The more I softened into this truth, the more connected our household became. I no longer needed to dominate or direct. I could listen more. Allow more. Hold more space. And because of that, my relationship with each of my children deepened in ways I hadn't known were possible.

My conversations with Andrés began to evolve. What used to be quick exchanges turned into long, thoughtful dialogues about school, friendships, sports, life questions. He began approaching me not just for answers, but for presence. Because he felt I was truly there. He felt my attention. He felt my willingness to listen without trying to fix. He felt that I saw him. And there is no gift more important to a child than feeling seen.

Cruz, with his passionate, expressive nature, taught me how to hold space for big emotions without absorbing them. He taught me how to be steady without shutting him down. How to give him permission to feel without rushing him to "move on." He made me more patient. More compassionate. More attuned.

And Luna, with her sensitivity and intuitive heart, showed me how energy moves through a family. She showed me how quickly she mirrors my state. How deeply she senses disconnection. How easily she opens when she feels safe. She taught me that softness is not weakness—it is wisdom. She became one of my greatest teachers in emotional literacy.

As I started applying the Map of Consciousness to my home life, everything became clearer. I could sense the difference between interactions happening at the frequency of pride versus courage. I could see how quickly fear lowered the collective energy of the house. I could feel how forgiveness lifted everything instantly. I could see how shame—especially self-shame—closed doors, while love opened them.

And I began to understand something fundamental: a home is not built through rules. It is built through frequency.

The frequency of the adults sets the tone. The frequency of the environment sets the safety. The frequency of the rituals sets the rhythm. The frequency of the conversations sets the culture.

A home is its own ecosystem. And like any ecosystem, it responds to attention, energy, and intention.

One evening, after a long and tiring workweek, I came home overwhelmed and mentally overloaded. Everyone was at the dinner table, but the energy felt disconnected—small annoyances, tired tones, short responses. I felt myself slipping into impatience. Then I remembered something I had learned through Sanctum: shift the energy, not the conversation. So I stood up, took a deep breath, softened my posture, and said gently, "Okay. Let's reset. Everyone, take one deep breath with me." The kids laughed, Jessica smiled, and for a moment the whole room softened. That one breath changed the entire energy of the night. Not because the breath was magical—but because intention was.

Small acts of presence become architecture. They become gravitational fields. They become anchors.

We started establishing rituals—tiny, consistent gestures that gave our home rhythm and warmth. A gratitude ritual before bed. Music as the emotional thermostat. The Koala Moon meditations that lulled the kids into sleep. Family walks. Eye contact. Hugging long enough for nervous systems to match. These were not performances—they were practices. They built emotional safety. They created attachment. They created connection.

Over time, I began to see how conscious hospitality was not something I practiced only at work. It was something I lived. Everywhere. With everyone. Especially the people I loved most.

It also reshaped my relationship with my parents. As I practiced emotional regulation, presence, and empathy at home, I found myself able to revisit my childhood from a different frequency. I could see the pain my mother carried. The battles my father lost silently. I could see how their trauma shaped their parenting. I could feel compassion where I once felt judgment. And from that frequency of compassion, something miraculous happened—our relationship softened. Hard conversations became possible. Honesty became easier. Forgiveness became a doorway rather than a barrier.

Children learn forgiveness from us. Partners experience it with us. Parents are liberated by it. And we are healed through it.

This is the essence of integration at home: living from the frequencies you want your family to inherit. Not through speeches or rules, but through nervous system leadership. Through choice. Through presence. Through alignment.

A home does not need perfection. It needs coherence.

It needs a leader who knows when to lead and when to follow. It needs a parent who knows when to speak and when to listen. It needs a partner who knows when to stand firm and when to soften. It needs rituals that elevate. Conversations that heal. Moments that bring everyone back to center.

Above all, it needs love—not conceptual, performative love, but embodied, attentive, grounded love. Love that can sit in the mess. Love that can listen through the discomfort. Love that can breathe through the tension. Love that can forgive. Love that can stay.

This is Conscious Hospitality at home. Not service. Not performance. Not technique. But **being**. Being attuned. Being present. Being aligned. Being intentional. Being empathetic. Being aware of the frequencies running through the people you love.

It is the leadership that matters most—not because it is the hardest, but because it is the most sacred.

PRACTICES OF CONSCIOUS HOSPITALITY AT HOME

Practices of Presence at Home

1. Put your phone away for the first thirty minutes after arriving home.

2. Offer one uninterrupted moment of full presence to each family member every day.

3. Practice one family grounding ritual—deep breaths, eye contact, or gratitude.

4. Slow your voice. Slow your pace. Slow your reactions.

5. Notice your energy before you walk into a room and adjust as needed.

REFLECTION: SEEING YOUR HOME WITH NEW EYES

- How would I describe the energy I bring home each night?
- Where do I rush when I should be listening?
- Where does my presence uplift—and where does it unintentionally contract?
- How do my children experience me? How does my partner experience me?
- Where am I living my values at home, and where am I performing them?

DO THE WORK: EMBODYING CONSCIOUS LEADERSHIP AT HOME

1. Establish a weekly family ritual (dinner, walk, gratitude circle).

2. Choose one nightly ritual to anchor connection (storytime, meditation, reflection).

3. Apologize quickly and sincerely when you misstep.

4. Schedule one hour per week of intentional one-on-one time with each child.

5. Create a shared "family values" list and revisit it monthly.

As our home became more aligned, something quiet but powerful began to unfold. The more I anchored presence, intention, authenticity, and empathy with Jessica and the kids, the more my entire life recalibrated. Home softened me. It centered me. It showed me what real connection felt like—connection without performance, without pressure, without the need to prove anything.

And as this coherence grew, I noticed a shift in myself. I was leading differently at work, listening more deeply, reacting less. I wasn't striving to be in control; I was choosing to be in service. The energy I cultivated at home began shaping the energy I carried everywhere else. For the first time, leadership didn't feel like something I *did*—it felt like something I *was*.

That's when a deeper question started forming inside me:
What is leadership for, if not to love?

Not sentimental love, but love expressed as presence, clarity, care, and integrity. Love as the quiet intention to leave every room better than you found it. Love as the impulse to lift others, not through words or authority, but through energy.

I didn't fully grasp it then, but I could feel it—a gentle pull toward something beyond efficiency, beyond success, beyond advancement. My home had become my teacher, and now life was asking me to bring what I had learned into the world in a new way.

That question—*How does love move through leadership?*—marked the beginning of my next awakening. A turning point that arrived not through crisis, but through subtle misalignment. Not through loss, but through evolution.

The next chapter is the story of that shift—the moment when presence became purpose, when service became impact, and when consciousness transformed into movement.

CHAPTER 12
Love in Action

"The best way to find yourself is to lose yourself in the service of others."
—Mahatma Gandhi

There came a season in my life when everything at home felt beautifully whole—deep, steady, resonant. Jessica and I were more connected than ever, the kind of connection that comes not from effort but from awareness. The kids were thriving, each in their own way, their personalities unfolding in real time, inviting me into their worlds with a purity I hadn't always been present enough to recognize. Our days were filled with small rituals, shared meals, playful chaos, bedtime conversations, and that quiet comfort that comes from living in coherence with the people you love. For the first time, I felt the long-sought harmony that had eluded me for years—an alignment between my inner world and my outer life.

So when the opportunity came to step into a global role that allowed me to live in Ibiza, remain with my family, and travel the world doing work I believed in, it felt like life was opening a new chapter. Purpose and family no longer felt at odds. Instead, they felt like two sides of the same truth finally moving in the same direction. I believed I had reached the peak of balance; the culmination of years of inner work.

Yet even the most conscious path can still invite new lessons. Sometimes growth doesn't arrive through crisis or disruption, but through subtle shifts—small, nearly invisible changes in rhythm that begin to whisper that something inside you is evolving faster than the life around you. It was in this quiet space that I began to experience what would become my second reckoning.

For a long time, I believed presence was the destination. If I could master my attention, I thought, I could master my life. That was my first awakening. But presence alone, I would learn, means little if it does not move others. Awareness is powerful, but awareness without impact is insight without purpose.

This truth revealed itself during my time as the global COO of Nômade People.

It was 2022, and we were pioneering a new vision of hospitality—spaces designed not just to host people, but to awaken something in them; places where community was created through emotion, where connection was not scripted but felt. It was everything I had dreamed of throughout my career: creativity, innovation, global reach, the opportunity to redefine what hospitality could be. I was based in Ibiza, traveling constantly between Mexico, the U.S., and Europe. I spent my days shaping new concepts, coaching teams, aligning operations, and helping build something that felt beautifully human.

My routines were disciplined and sacred. I meditated every morning. I fasted on flights and used the long hours in the sky as moments of introspection. I devoured books on consciousness, physics, spirituality, and human potential. I was living a life I had crafted with intention, and for a while, it felt deeply aligned.

But slowly, almost imperceptibly at first, something shifted.

Meetings that once flowed began to feel heavy. Decisions that once came intuitively became effortful. Ideas I would have once felt energized by now landed softly, without resonance. Nothing was "wrong" in any obvious way. But something in me knew that the energetic match I had once felt was no longer there. I could sense myself changing, and the environment around me no longer met me where I was evolving into.

It wasn't burnout. It wasn't disillusionment. It was misalignment—a subtle but unmistakable drift between what I was doing and who I was becoming. And misalignment has its own frequency. It doesn't shout; it whispers. It unsettles rather than disrupts.

I tried to compensate. I worked harder. I organized more. I tightened my routines. I deepened my practices. But effort cannot force alignment. And what had once been flow began to feel like swimming against a slow but persistent current.

The truth is simple: when your inner frequency shifts and your external world does not shift with it, friction follows. You feel yourself moving in one direction while your environment anchors you to another. And no amount of discipline can override that quiet but clear call to evolve.

The realization crystallized late one night in a hotel room in Mexico City after a week of back-to-back meetings across three time zones. The room was serene—a calm, minimalist space with soft lighting and clean lines. But for the first time, it felt hollow. I closed my laptop, stared at the ceiling, and whispered a question to myself that came from the deepest part of my being:

Is this it?

That moment was not a crisis. It was clarity. For years, I had measured progress by motion—how far, how fast, how high. But I suddenly saw the truth with painful simplicity: movement without meaning is just movement. Success without service is empty. Position without impact is superficial. And leadership without love is noise.

True fulfillment does not come from how much you achieve, but from how deeply your presence elevates the people around you. Impact, I understood in that moment, is nothing more than love in action. Not romantic love, not sentimental love, but energetic love—care expressed through leadership, generosity expressed through presence, coherence expressed through service.

I realized I couldn't remain in a role simply because it looked aligned on paper. My life was asking me to step into something deeper, more honest, more resonant. And so, even though I didn't yet know exactly what I was moving toward, I knew I had to move.

That was the night Conscious Hospitality Unlimited was born—not as a business plan, not as a brand, but as a calling. A promise to bring together consciousness, leadership, and humanity in a way that touched people, not just organizations. A commitment to remind leaders that the most advanced technology on Earth remains the human heart—and that leadership begins, always, with energy.

In the early months, I worked obsessively—not out of pressure, but out of devotion. I poured myself into creating a framework that could translate presence, authenticity, intention, and empathy into tangible results. But even more importantly, I focused on helping people feel again. To care again. To remember that leadership is not efficiency, but connection.

There was one morning, early in this chapter, that stays with me. I was consulting for a resort in southern Europe, arriving before sunrise, walking through the back corridors toward the kitchen. The tension in the air was thick—voices raised, plates stacking up, frustration visible in every movement. The old version of me would have stepped in with structure and correction.

But this time, I tied on an apron and stepped into the line. For a moment, we worked in silence. Then someone cracked a joke. Music began to play. Shoulders softened. The energy of the room transformed—not through instruction, but through presence.

That morning reinforced what I had been circling for years: leadership is not what you say. Leadership is what you transmit. When you are grounded, people around you ground. When you hold coherence, rooms reorganize around it. When you care deeply, others begin to care too.

This is love in action—not a concept, not a gesture, but a way of being. It is the subtle force that softens the edges of conflict, lifts the weight from a team, creates safety in uncertainty, and turns routine moments into human ones. Love in action is not sentimental; it is responsible. It is the highest expression of leadership.

Today, as both the founder of Conscious Hospitality Unlimited and a leader within an organization once again, I carry this philosophy into every space I enter—whether I'm speaking to a team, welcoming guests, coaching an executive, settling into a plane seat before a long flight, or sitting with my children at the dinner table. Jessica and I speak often about how our definition of success has changed. For years, success was movement. Now, it is depth. It is presence. It is alignment. It is how connected we feel to ourselves and to the people who matter most.

Andrés, Cruz, and Luna continue to be my greatest teachers. They pull me back into presence with their curiosity, their questions, their honesty. They remind me that Conscious Hospitality begins at home. It begins with love. It begins with awareness.

Looking back, I see how each awakening prepared me for the next. The first taught me attention. The second taught me purpose. This one taught me peace—not stillness, but coherence; not perfection, but alignment; not achievement, but resonance.

This, ultimately, is the heart of Conscious Hospitality. It is not a business framework. It is not a methodology. It is a way of being. It is the decision, moment after moment, to let awareness become love and love become movement. When you lead this way, every interaction becomes meaningful. Every moment becomes an invitation. Every room becomes a place of connection. And every act, no matter how small, becomes a chance to serve.

This is love in action. And perhaps this is what consciousness has been asking of us all along—to remember that the smallest acts of grace are often the ones that move the world forward.

As this journey unfolded, I began to recognize a deeper pattern: every lesson in leadership, every moment of presence at work or at home, ultimately traced back to one central truth—knowing yourself. The energy you carry, the awareness you cultivate, the intentions you embody, the choices you make all flow from the clarity of your inner blueprint. The experiences with my teams, my family, and within myself revealed that transformation is not about learning something new; it is about remembering who you are beneath the layers of conditioning, expectation, and habit.

And so the next chapter of this work invites you inward—to map the architecture of your own nature, your values, your fears, your patterns, your gifts, your alignment. This is the beginning of *The Blueprint*, the foundation upon which conscious leadership, conscious parenting, and conscious living are built. Here, the principles we've explored take form, holding space for your presence to ripple outward with clarity, resonance, and love.

CHAPTER 13
The Conscious Blueprint

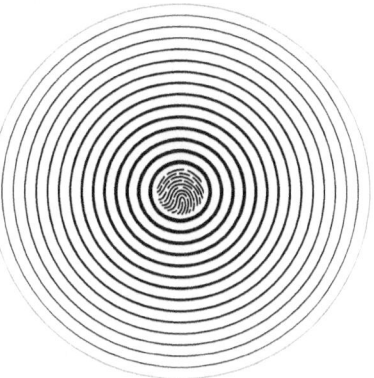

"Knowing yourself is the beginning of all wisdom."
—Aristotle

The image at the center of the Conscious Hospitality mark was never intended to be decorative. It was placed there as a quiet acknowledgement of something most of us sense long before we have language for it: that each human being carries a pattern that is entirely their own, and that this pattern moves through the world whether we are aware of it or not. A fingerprint is not something we design, refine, or improve. It is formed before preference, before ambition, before identity has had time to assemble itself. Its ridges and whorls are fixed by nature, not choice, and yet they become a point of contact with everything we touch. They leave traces. They receive information. They participate in the world intimately, personally, without effort or intention.

In the same way, each of us carries an energetic imprint. We arrive everywhere with it. It enters rooms before we speak. It shapes conversations before decisions are made. It influences how others feel in our presence long before strategy, language, or behavior come online. This imprint is not something we turn on or off. It is not something we manage well on good days and poorly on bad ones. It is simply what is being transmitted when we are being ourselves, for better or worse. This is not symbolism or abstraction. It is the lived substrate beneath leadership, hospitality, parenting, and relationship. What we transmit is always more than what we intend.

I became aware of this most clearly during a quiet moment in Mexico, sitting alone on the terrace of a small resort after years of leading teams across continents. By that point in my career, I had spent decades refining systems— operational excellence, guest experience, leadership frameworks that were thoughtful, rigorous, and effective. They delivered results. They created consistency. They allowed organizations to scale and people to perform under pressure. And yet, when I looked back at the moments that truly shaped culture, morale, and momentum, they were not the ones where the framework worked perfectly. They were the moments where something subtler was at play. Moments where a conversation softened without explanation, where a team steadied without instruction, where complexity seemed to resolve itself not through force or authority, but through tone.

I began to notice that when my internal state was coherent, the environment responded differently. Decisions clarified more quickly. Friction eased. People felt held without being managed. When that coherence was missing, effort increased—even when outcomes looked successful on the surface. The work still got done, but it cost more. More energy. More vigilance. More self-management. That was when the fingerprint revealed itself not as a symbol, but as architecture. As something structural. As something that organizes experience from the inside out.

Much of this book has explored how presence, authenticity, intention, empathy, and integration shape the quality of experience. These principles matter deeply. They support progress. They help us lead with greater care, relate with more honesty, and take responsibility for the impact we have on others. For many people, this work is genuinely transformative in a practical sense. It improves how life is lived. It refines how leadership is expressed. It brings consciousness into moments that once ran on autopilot. And yet, over time, something else became clear to me.

Many people were progressing, but something essential remained unchanged. They were becoming more capable, more aware, more articulate—while continuing to live from the same internal center. The same identity structures. The same nervous system patterns. The same relationship to effort and control. The self was becoming more refined, but it was still doing the work of holding everything together. Progress improved the experience of being that self. Transformation reorganized what was doing the living in the first place.

Transformation follows an order, whether we recognize it or not. There is an architecture to change, just as there is an architecture to buildings, ecosystems, and organizations. When that architecture remains unseen, growth becomes tiring. Insight accumulates without relief. Practices multiply without integration. People become increasingly self-aware, yet feel no more at ease inside their own lives. This is not a failure of intelligence or sincerity. It is not a lack of discipline or commitment. It is structural. Something fundamental is being asked to change without the conditions being in place for that change to stabilize.

Beneath everything we do lives a system—a living system that determines whether awareness feels spacious or overwhelming, whether insight settles or destabilizes, whether leadership feels grounding or draining. This system is not linear. It does not respond well to sequencing or force. It functions dimensionally. Each layer organizes the one beneath it. Each dimension sets the conditions for what can follow. When these layers align, life feels coherent. There is less internal conflict, less unnecessary effort, less need to manage oneself constantly. When they do not align, effort increases—not because something is wrong, but because the system is compensating.

This recognition became the foundation of what I came to call *The Conscious Blueprint*.

The Conscious Blueprint is not a ladder to climb or a checklist to complete. It is not a set of steps designed to get you somewhere else. It is a dimensional framework for transformation, one that reflects how change actually becomes livable. Awareness allows us to see without immediately reacting or fixing. Regulation allows the body to soften enough for awareness to land. Coherence emerges when the system stops working against itself. Embodiment is where truth becomes behavior, especially under pressure. These are not concepts to master or ideas to collect. They are states that must be lived.

Conscious Hospitality revealed how presence changes everything. It showed that leadership, service, and relationship are shaped less by technique than by the quality of being we bring into the moment. The Conscious Blueprint explores what allows that presence to endure. It turns toward the architecture beneath effort, identity, and control—toward the nervous system, attention, energy, and integration. Toward the invisible structures that determine whether leadership replenishes or depletes, whether care feels natural or costly, whether responsibility feels spacious or heavy.

This is not a departure from hospitality. It is its maturation. Hospitality, at its deepest level, is not something we perform. It is something we transmit. And transmission is only as clean as the system doing the transmitting.

When the Blueprint is honored, leadership simplifies. Decisions clarify. Repair happens more quickly. Presence no longer needs to be maintained through effort. This is true in organizations and families alike. It is true in moments of visibility and in moments no one else sees. The fingerprint does not change. What changes is our relationship to it.

This chapter is not meant as an ending. It is a threshold. An acknowledgment that presence alone cannot override exhaustion, and that intention alone cannot reorganize a system structured around vigilance and control. *The Conscious Blueprint: The Architecture Beneath Effort, Identity, and Control* is the next evolution of this work. It does not add more to do. It looks more deeply at what is already doing the living.

And when that understanding becomes embodied rather than conceptual, hospitality stops being something we practice. It becomes the natural expression of a system finally at ease with itself.

Conclusion

To you—the reader, the leader, the human on this path—thank you. Thank you for walking with me through these pages, for staying open to reflection, and for being willing to look inward before reaching outward. For choosing consciousness in a world that so often rewards distraction and numbness. For remembering that leadership begins with presence—and presence begins with truth.

This book is not an ending. It is a beginning. A beginning of a life lived with intentionality. A beginning of deeper connection—to yourself, to your teams, to your family, and to your community. A beginning of offering your energy to the world with clarity, purpose, and love.

As you move forward, carry this understanding: the world doesn't need more strategy, more hustle, or more perfection. It needs people who can show up fully, who can regulate themselves before trying to lead others, who can anchor energy in moments of uncertainty, and who can model the power of care in action.

The greatest differentiator for tomorrow's leaders will not be knowledge or speed—it will be coherence. The ability to align mind, heart, and presence, and to transmit that alignment into every interaction. When your energy is steady, authentic, and grounded, you become the compass for those around you. You create a field where others feel safe to grow, to experiment, to be fully human. That is leadership. That is service. That is Conscious Hospitality.

Imagine the ripple effects of this approach: a team that works with ease rather than tension, a home that nurtures emotional intelligence and resilience, a community that is inspired by integrity and care. This is not abstract—it is possible, and it begins with you.

I wrote this book, in part, for my children—Andrés, Cruz, and Luna—and for the world they will grow into. I want them to inherit organizations that honor the whole person. I want them to walk into homes, schools, workplaces, and communities where the nervous system feels safe, where people are valued for their presence and integrity, not only their outputs. I want them to learn that the true measure of leadership is the impact we have on the lives, hearts, and energy of others.

I've already seen the early signals of this shift. I've seen teams pause to breathe together before meetings. I've seen leaders ask, "How are you really?"—and wait for the answer. I've seen hospitality teams choose presence over perfection, and I've watched the magic unfold. These are small, intentional acts, yet they create profound, systemic change.

The butterfly is emerging. The cocoon is cracking. The evolution is underway. A conscious host is anyone who chooses to show up fully:

- At the dinner table, engaging with presence.
- In the boardroom, leading with clarity and care.
- On a morning walk, noticing and connecting with life.
- In welcoming a partner home, or a guest into your space.
- In holding space for a struggling team member.
- In caring for yourself, even when no one is watching.

To host consciously is to stand as a lighthouse—grounded, aware, and intentional—in a world still seeking its center. To embody the truth that service is sacred, and leadership is energy in motion.

One night, after a long day, I was putting Luna to bed. I was distracted, replaying conversations, already planning the next day. She looked at me and said softly:

"Papi, I like when you're not in a hurry."

It stopped me cold. That's what people want—everywhere. In our homes, in our teams, in our hearts. To not be hurried. To feel seen. To feel safe.

That is the ultimate luxury. That is Conscious Hospitality. And that is the kind of world we can create—together.

May you lead with presence.
May you serve with soul.
May you speak with intention.
May you love with coherence.

And may your life—in every room, every role, every breath—be an act of Conscious Hospitality.

The evolution is here. The butterfly has wings. Now, let us rise—together.

—David

The Conscious Living Library

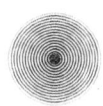

Books have always been my closest companions. I grew up in a home where words lived everywhere—on nightstands, beside the sofa, and in my parents' hands late into the night.

My father read incessantly. From him, I learned that immersing yourself in a good book is like traveling to new places, meeting people you've never met, and living lives you've never lived. He taught me that stories expand not only your imagination, but your humanity. His love for calligraphy, for the beauty of language, and for the elegance of expression planted in me a lifelong passion for writing.

From my mother, I learned that books hold the keys to life's most important questions. She taught me that seeking is not weakness—it's courage. That answers aren't fixed but discovered through experience. She showed me that life is multidimensional—emotional, spiritual, and intellectual all at once—and that curiosity is how we grow into the fullness of our being.

From both of them, I inherited a love for words, for reflection, and for the quiet companionship of ideas. Creativity, curiosity, and the discipline to keep learning were not lessons; they were the air we breathed at home.

As I grew, so did my library. My friends and mentors became part of it too. To this day, everyone in my close circle has a book from me—usually with a handwritten note inside. Gifting books has always felt like the most personal way to share what has shaped me. It's a conversation that never ends.

Over the years, certain books, podcasts, and teachings have accompanied me through every season—helping me see more clearly, lead more consciously, and live more intentionally. The right book always seemed to arrive at the right moment, each one leaving an imprint that eventually became part of *Conscious Hospitality*.

PRESENCE, AWARENESS, AND CONSCIOUSNESS

Before anything else, consciousness begins with presence — the quiet returning to yourself, the ongoing remembering of who you are beneath all roles and responsibilities. These books shaped the foundation of my awareness. They helped me slow down, see more clearly, and understand the terrain of the inner world. Each one arrived at the exact moment I needed it and became part of the architecture of Conscious Hospitality.

Books That Fostered Presence

The Power of Now — Eckhart Tolle
This book gave me language for presence. It taught me that awareness is built in moments, not in theories, and that the present is the only place where clarity is found.

A New Earth — Eckhart Tolle
An expansion of consciousness framed through everyday life. It helped me understand the subtle ways the ego keeps us asleep, and how awakening is a choice we make repeatedly.

The Untethered Soul — Michael A. Singer
A guide to letting go of inner resistance. This book showed me how freedom begins with the courage to witness my thoughts rather than become them.

The Surrender Experiment — Michael A. Singer
A lived example of what happens when you trust life instead of trying to control it. It opened my heart to possibility and softened my attachment to outcomes.

Power vs. Force — David R. Hawkins
One of the foundations of my philosophy. It helped me understand that everything has a frequency — and that leadership is ultimately energetic.

Letting Go — David R. Hawkins
This book teaches a path of emotional release that feels like truth. It helped me see that compassion begins with lightening our inner load.

Becoming Supernatural — Dr. Joe Dispenza
A bridge between science and consciousness. It taught me the power of intention, coherence, and emotional regulation.

Breaking the Habit of Being Yourself—**Dr. Joe Dispenza**
A reminder that transformation is neurological. It showed me that change is possible when we take responsibility for our thinking.

Stillness is the Key—**Ryan Holiday**
A modern perspective on an ancient truth: stillness is strength. This book reinforced that leaders who slow down, see more.

The Artist's Way—**Julia Cameron**
A journey back to creativity through presence. It helped me return to writing as a form of awareness and healing.

The Practice—**Seth Godin**
A reminder that presence is not passive—it is a discipline. Godin helped me separate the noise from the signal.

The Mountain is You—**Brianna Wiest**
A powerful guide to self-sabotage and self-awareness. It gave me language for the ways we unconsciously block our own growth.

In Love With the World—**Yongey Mingyur Rinpoche**
A profound story of spiritual awakening. It reminded me that presence is the art of meeting each moment with openness.

Wherever You Go, There You Are—**Jon Kabat-Zinn**
A practical meditation companion that grounded my understanding of mindfulness in daily life.

The Kybalion—**Three Initiates**
Hermetic principles that expanded my view of consciousness as a universal structure. Subtle, profound, and deeply influential.

The Impersonal Life—**Joseph Benner**
A humbling reminder that ego is not identity. This book helped me refine my relationship with responsibility and purpose.

The Power of Awareness—**Neville Goddard**
A transformative understanding of imagination as a creative force. It helped me see the link between belief and manifestation.

Awareness—**Anthony de Mello**
A call to wake up. Simple, sharp truths that pierce through illusion.

Podcast Episodes That Deepened Presence

Know Thyself Podcast—"The Power of Awareness" with Michael Singer
A masterclass in surrender and consciousness. It reaffirmed the necessity of releasing control in leadership and life.

Sanctum: Mindful Movement—Conversation with Luuk Melisse
This experience at Six Senses Ibiza transformed the way I understand awareness in the body. Sanctum taught me that presence is a full-body practice—breath, movement, sound, and community coming together to awaken the self.

Know Thyself Podcast—"Healing the Nervous System"
with Dr. Joe Dispenza
A powerful dialogue about coherence, emotional mastery, and the biology of change.

The Higher Self With Danny Morel—"Your True Essence"
Danny's teachings helped me connect presence with identity. This episode reminded me that our highest self can only be accessed in stillness.

Huberman Lab—"How to Improve Focus and Resist Distraction"
A scientific explanation of presence, giving me tools to manage my attention as a leader.

Films and Documentaries That Expand Awareness

Awake: The Life of Yogananda
A reminder that presence is a path of devotion—to self-realization, to practice, to love.

The Mind, Explained
Insightful episodes on mindfulness, anxiety, and consciousness that bridge science and human experience.

Heal
A powerful exploration of the mind-body connection and the emotional roots of physical healing.

InnSaei—The Power of Intuition
A beautiful look at inner knowing. This film helped me trust the felt sense that guides leadership.

Talks and Speeches

Eckhart Tolle—"The Depth of Stillness"
A reminder that presence deepens as noise quiets. This talk brought me back to myself countless times.

Oprah Winfrey—"Super Soul Sunday"
Conversations that reveal the heart of awareness and emotional honesty.

Michael Singer—"Experiencing the Soul"
A profound lecture on consciousness and the seat of awareness.

LEADERSHIP AND HUMAN DYNAMICS

Leadership, at its deepest level, is the art of understanding people—their motivations, fears, potential, strengths, wounds, and the way their energy shapes the room. These are the books, ideas, and voices that helped me evolve from managing tasks to elevating human beings; from controlling outcomes to cultivating environments where people thrive.

Across all my years in global hospitality—from New York to Hawaii, Hong Kong to Ibiza—these works gave me language for things I intuitively felt. They helped me build stronger teams, ask better questions, navigate complexity, and grow into the kind of leader I always wished I'd had early in my career.

This section blends classic leadership teachings, modern behavioral insights, psychological frameworks, human-centered approaches, and stories of transformation that have stayed with me for life.

Books That Shaped My Leadership

The 7 Habits of Highly Effective People—**Stephen R. Covey**
Covey taught me that leadership begins with inner mastery. This book helped me shift from being reactive to being intentional—from managing circumstances to choosing who I wanted to be.

Principle-Centered Leadership—**Stephen R. Covey**
A timeless reminder that true leadership is rooted in timeless values, not trends or tactics.

Good to Great—Jim Collins
A foundational work that taught me humility is the highest form of leadership—and that character always outperforms charisma.

Leaders Eat Last—Simon Sinek
This book gave language to the instinct I always carried: people perform at their best when they feel safe, seen, and supported.

Start with Why—Simon Sinek
Purpose creates belonging. This book helped me understand that clarity is one of the greatest gifts a leader can give.

Dare to Lead—Brené Brown
A shift in leadership culture: vulnerability as strength, courage as practice, and emotional honesty as a prerequisite for trust.

The Five Dysfunctions of a Team—Patrick Lencioni
A mirror for every leader. It showed me that performance issues are almost always the result of relational issues—trust, communication, accountability.

Multipliers—Liz Wiseman
A powerful reminder that great leaders expand the intelligence and capability of those around them. It helped me stop over-functioning and start empowering.

What Got You Here Won't Get You There—Marshall Goldsmith
A humbling, necessary guide that showed me leadership evolution requires unlearning old patterns—especially the ones that made you successful in the first place.

The Culture Code—Daniel Coyle
A blueprint for building environments of safety, trust, and belonging—the core ingredients of high-performing teams.

Drive—Daniel Pink
A clear explanation of what truly motivates people: mastery, autonomy, purpose. It changed the way I structured team expectations.

Radical Candor—Kim Scott
A reminder that clarity is kindness, and courageous conversations are acts of care.

Extreme Ownership—**Jocko Willink and Leif Babin**
This book sharpened my understanding of responsibility and taught me the
discipline of ownership without blame.

The Advantage—**Patrick Lencioni**
A guide to organizational health—the often invisible foundation of
business success.

Atomic Habits—**James Clear**
Leadership is habit. Culture is habit. Excellence is habit. This book gave
me practical methods to build consistency in teams and self.

Mindset—**Carol Dweck**
A reminder that every great leader is rooted in a growth mindset—the
willingness to evolve, learn, and adapt.

Turn the Ship Around!—**David Marquet**
A radical shift from command-and-control to leader-leader. A must-read in
hospitality, where empowerment creates magic.

Management Mess to Leadership Success—**Scott Jeffrey Miller**
A refreshing and vulnerable take on leadership. Scott's humility taught me
that great leaders grow through their mistakes, not despite them.

PSYCHOLOGY, HUMAN BEHAVIOR, AND TEAM DYNAMICS

Foundational Readings on the Human Experience

Emotional Intelligence—**Daniel Goleman**
One of the most important leadership books I've ever read. It helped me
understand that awareness and empathy are not soft skills—they are the
foundation of human effectiveness.

The Fearless Organization—**Amy Edmondson**
A deep dive into psychological safety and why it matters more than strategy,
talent, or experience.

Crucial Conversations—**Patterson, Grenny, McMillan, Switzler**
A toolkit for navigating high-stakes conversations with clarity and care.

Quiet—**Susan Cain**
This book changed the way I lead introverts. It taught me to value the quiet wisdom in the room.

The Coaching Habit—**Michael Bungay Stanier**
A reminder that great leadership is about asking, not telling.

Thanks for the Feedback—**Douglas Stone and Sheila Heen**
Helped me understand feedback as a relationship, not a transaction.

Difficult Conversations—**Stone, Patton and Heen**
Equipped me with language to approach conflict with empathy instead of fear.

The Infinite Game—**Simon Sinek**
A shift from short-term wins to long-term legacy.

Podcasts and Episodes That Shaped My Leadership

On Leadership with Scott Miller—**Various Episodes**
Scott's ability to translate leadership into daily actions has shaped my own coaching and development style.

Know Thyself Podcast—**"Emotional Mastery and Secure Leadership" with Dr. Nicole LePera**
A powerful conversation on nervous system awareness and how leaders can cultivate emotional regulation.

Tim Ferriss Show—**"Jim Collins: The Return"**
An extraordinary dialogue on discipline, humility, and leadership as service.

Huberman Lab—**"The Science of Productivity and Focus"**
An essential resource for leaders seeking to master their attention and energy.

The Higher Self With Danny Morel — **"The Power of Internal Leadership"**
A reminder that external leadership begins with internal clarity.

Brené Brown — "Daring Leadership"
A grounding episode on vulnerability, courage, and culture.

Films and Documentaries That Expand Leadership Insight

Jiro Dreams of Sushi
A masterclass in craftsmanship, mastery, humility, and devotion to excellence—everything leadership should be.

The Last Dance
A raw look at leadership dynamics, ego, team psychology, and the cost of greatness.

Chef's Table
Stories of vision, discipline, artistry, and the tension between perfection and humanity.

The Playbook
Coaches revealing the philosophies behind winning and team culture.

Talks and Speeches That Shifted My Leadership

Simon Sinek — "How Great Leaders Inspire Action" (TED)
A timeless reminder that people follow purpose, not power.

Angela Duckworth — "Grit" (TED)
A transformative perspective on perseverance and passion.

Admiral William McRaven — "Make Your Bed"
A beautiful reminder that leadership begins with discipline in the smallest actions.

Brené Brown — "The Power of Vulnerability" (TED)
A turning point in global leadership thinking.

ENERGY, NEUROSCIENCE AND HUMAN POTENTIAL

Human potential expands when energy, intention, and biology come into alignment. These are the works that helped me understand the inner mechanics of change—how thoughts shape chemistry, how emotions shape action, how the nervous system shapes presence, and how coherence shapes consciousness.

This section bridges science and spirit. It reflects a truth I've lived and witnessed across the world: when leaders regulate their internal state, everything around them changes.

These books, studies, and conversations helped me understand the nervous system, the brain, the subconscious, trauma, habit loops, coherence, and the energetic nature of human beings. They shaped the way I lead teams, guide people, support transformation, and connect with myself.

Books That Expanded My Understanding of Human Potential

Becoming Supernatural—**Dr. Joe Dispenza**
A groundbreaking book that helped me understand coherence, brain-wave states, and the biology of transformation. It gave scientific structure to what I was already experiencing internally.

Breaking the Habit of Being Yourself—**Dr. Joe Dispenza**
A clear reminder that our personality creates our personal reality. This book taught me that change is both neurological and emotional—and fully possible.

The Body Keeps the Score—**Bessel van der Kolk**
A powerful exploration of trauma, memory, and healing. It helped me understand my own emotional history and the emotional histories that every team carries into the workplace.

Why We Sleep—**Matthew Walker**
This book changed the way I think about recovery, creativity, emotional regulation, and leadership performance.

Peak Mind—**Amishi Jha**
A practical guide to training attention. It showed me that focus is not a personality trait—it's a trainable skill.

The Molecule of More—**Daniel Z. Lieberman and Michael E. Long**
A fascinating look at dopamine and desire. It helped me understand modern distraction and the "chasing" behavior that keeps leaders exhausted.

The Rise of Superman—**Steven Kotler**
A deep dive into flow states—and how humans access peak performance through presence and full engagement.

Flow—**Mihaly Csikszentmihalyi**
The original research behind the concept of flow. It helped me see why mastery requires the merging of challenge and skill.

The Talent Code—**Daniel Coyle**
A powerful explanation of deep practice and myelin—the literal wiring of talent.

The Source—**Tara Swart**
A neuroscience-based look at manifestation, intuition, and the mind-body connection.

The HeartMath Solution—**Doc Childre and Howard Martin**
A system that changed my life. Heart coherence, emotional regulation, and the power of the heart's electromagnetic field became foundational to my understanding of conscious leadership.

The Biology of Belief—**Dr. Bruce Lipton**
A paradigm-shifting book that connects belief systems with cellular biology. It helped me see how deeply we shape our own reality.

Books on Energy, Emotion and the Subtle Body

Eastern Body, Western Mind—**Anodea Judith**
A bridge between spirituality and psychology. This book helped me understand emotional patterns through the lens of the energy centers.

The Energy Codes—**Dr. Sue Morter**
A beautiful guide to embodiment and energetic wholeness.

Frequency—**Penney Peirce**
A reminder that everything—thoughts, emotions, people, rooms—
carries vibration.

The Subtle Body—**Cyndi Dale**
A deep, comprehensive map of energetic anatomy.

Waking the Tiger—**Peter A. Levine**
A powerful explanation of trauma, energy, and the instinctive body's role
in healing.

Podcasts and Episodes That Raised My Capacity

Huberman Lab—**"The Science of Emotions, Stress, and Resilience"**
Andrew Huberman brings clarity to how the nervous system operates
during stress—giving leaders tools to stay grounded.

Huberman Lab—**"Using the Brain-Body Contract
to Improve Focus and Presence"**
A masterclass in energy management. This episode changed how I prepare
for meetings, decisions, and demanding days.

Know Thyself Podcast—**"Healing the Nervous System and Embodiment"
with Irene Lyon**
A profound conversation about regulation, trauma, and inner safety—
essential for conscious leadership.

Know Thyself Podcast—**"Transcending the Mind"
with Dr. Joe Dispenza**
One of the clearest explanations of meditation, coherence, and
human potential.

Know Thyself Podcast—**"Awakening the Body's Intelligence"
with Thomas Hübl**
This conversation helped me understand collective trauma and
group coherence.

Sanctum: Mindful Movement—with Luuk Melisse
(Sanctum origin story and the power of embodied presence)
A deeply meaningful episode for me personally. Sanctum integrates breath, movement, ritual, and spirituality into a single experience. It taught me that awareness is physical, emotional, and communal.

The Higher Self With Danny Morel—**"The Awakening"**
A conversation tht connected human potential with spiritual alignment. Danny's way of speaking about truth, awareness, and inner healing shaped my own practices.

Ten Percent Happier—**"How to Train Your Brain for Calm and Clarity" with Amishi Jha**
A practical guide to mindfulness for high-performing leaders.

The Rich Roll Podcast—**"The Science of Flow" with Steven Kotler**
A brilliant exploration of peak performance and the states that produce extraordinary results.

Documentaries and Films That Opened My Awareness

Heal
A documentary that reframed the mind-body connection in a powerful, hopeful way.

Limitless with Chris Hemsworth
A beautiful exploration of aging, longevity, resilience, fear, and human potential.

Stutz
A raw, intimate documentary on tools for emotional mastery—beautifully human and profoundly practical.

Fantastic Fungi
An exploration of nature's intelligence, interconnectedness, and the healing potential of altered states.

The Wisdom of Trauma—Gabor Maté
A documentary that changed my perspective on suffering and compassion.

InnSaei—The Power of Intuition
A film that revealed the intelligence beneath thought.

Talks, Teachings and Moments That Shifted My Perspective

Dr. Joe Dispenza—"The Formula for Change"
A clear, practical explanation of how thoughts create outcomes.

Gabor Maté—"The Power of Emotional Truth"
A talk that anchored my understanding of compassion and internal safety.

Deepak Chopra—"The Future of Wellbeing"
A merging of science, spirituality, and human potential.

Gregg Braden—"The Power of Heart Intelligence"
A profound exploration of coherence and human connectivity.

EMOTIONAL HEALING AND INNER WORK

You cannot lead others beyond the depth to which you've led yourself. And you cannot love others more deeply than the degree to which you've learned to soften toward your own story.

Leadership becomes conscious when we begin to do the inner work—when we examine our beliefs, our wounds, our fears, our conditioning, and the patterns we inherited long before we ever stepped into a leadership role.

These books, teachings, and conversations helped me understand the landscape of the emotional world: childhood patterns, nervous system imprints, forgiveness, compassion, shadow work, truth-telling, and the healing that happens when we stop running from ourselves.

This is the work that made me a better father, husband, leader, friend, and human being. It's also the work that allowed *Conscious Hospitality* to breathe into existence.

Books That Helped Me Heal, Release, and Rebuild From Within

A Return to Love—**Marianne Williamson**
A book that reframed forgiveness as the gateway to peace. It taught me that healing is not the erasing of the past but the release of its grip on the present.

A Course in Miracles—**Helen Schucman**
A lifelong journey in perception. It taught me that every moment offers

a choice between fear and love—and that forgiveness is the bridge between the two.

The Gifts of Imperfection—Brené Brown
A permission slip to be human. This book helped me release perfectionism and embrace authenticity as strength.

Daring Greatly—Brené Brown
An invitation to courage. It helped me understand vulnerability as the foundation for connection, both at work and at home.

Atlas of the Heart—Brené Brown
A map of emotions that gave me language for experiences I had carried for years. It helped me speak more honestly, even with myself.

The Power of Vulnerability—Brené Brown
This work taught me that healing begins with truth—the truth we tell ourselves and the truth we allow others to see.

The Mountain is You—Brianna Wiest
A powerful guide through self-sabotage, emotional patterns, and the internal mountains we are called to climb.

Attached—Amir Levine and Rachel Heller
This book helped me understand attachment styles—in leadership, relationships, parenting, and team dynamics.

No Bad Parts—Richard Schwartz
A transformative look at Internal Family Systems (IFS). It taught me compassion for the parts of myself that once felt broken.

The Body Keeps the Score—Bessel van der Kolk
A profound exploration of trauma and the way the body remembers. It helped me understand the emotional history I carried—and the emotional histories of the people I lead.

It Didn't Start With You—Mark Wolynn
A book that opened my eyes to inherited patterns—the emotional legacies passed through generations.

When the Body Says No—Gabor Maté
A masterclass in the connection between emotional suppression and physical illness. It helped me understand the cost of not telling ourselves the truth.

The Myth of Normal—Gabor Maté
A clear look at how society shapes emotional suffering. This book helped me understand compassion as an active practice.

Radical Acceptance—Tara Brach
A powerful reminder that healing begins with meeting yourself exactly where you are.

The Drama of the Gifted Child—Alice Miller
This book helped me understand how childhood roles form the emotional patterns that show up in our adult relationships and leadership.

The Four Agreements—Don Miguel Ruiz
Simple truths that anchor emotional freedom. A book I return to often.

Books on Shadow Work, Compassion and Emotional Truth

The Dark Side of the Light Chasers—Debbie Ford
A reminder that every shadow is a doorway to deeper wholeness.

Loving What Is—Byron Katie
A powerful process for questioning the thoughts that cause suffering.

The War of Art—Steven Pressfield
A raw look at resistance—the internal force that keeps us from stepping into our true self.

Your Body Knows the Score—Don St. John
A beautiful integration of somatic healing and emotional work.

Podcasts and Episodes That Deepened My Emotional Work

Know Thyself Podcast—"Healing Childhood Patterns"
with Dr. Nicole LePera
A clear explanation of generational wounding, self-regulation, and the emotional roots of behavior.

Know Thyself Podcast—"The Path of Forgiveness and Emotional Freedom" with Gabor Maté
A masterclass in compassion. This episode helped me understand that every emotional reaction has a story behind it.

The Higher Self With Danny More—**"Healing the Inner Child"**
A conversation that taught me the importance of seeing, validating, and loving the child within—the foundation of emotional wholeness.

On Purpose with Jay Shetty—**"How to Release What No Longer Serves You"**
A practical guide to emotional letting go.

The School of Greatness—**Lewis Howes and Gabor Maté**
A powerful exploration of shame, identity, and the healing power of truth.

Ten Percent Happier—**"Self-Compassion with Dr. Kristin Neff"**
A reminder that compassion begins with how we speak to ourselves.

Huberman Lab—**"Understanding Trauma and Emotional Regulation"**
A scientific lens on emotional healing that helped me understand my own patterns.

Documentaries and Films That Revealed the Human Heart

The Wisdom of Trauma—**Gabor Maté**
A film that opened a global conversation on pain, compassion, and the human condition.

Stutz—**Jonah Hill**
An intimate look into therapy, truth, grief, creativity, and the tools we use to heal.

Won't You Be My Neighbor (**Mr. Rogers documentary**)
A beautiful reminder of the healing power of kindness and presence.

The Mask You Live In
A documentary about masculinity, vulnerability, and the emotional conditioning of boys—deeply relevant to my own journey as a father.

Inside Out
A simple yet profound look into emotional processing—a story that has helped many adults and children name their feelings with compassion.

Talks, Teachings, and Wisdom That Shifted My Inner Landscape

Marianne Williamson—"The Power of Forgiveness"
A talk that helped me integrate forgiveness not as an idea but as a lived practice.

Eckhart Tolle—"How to Handle Emotional Pain"
A gentle reminder that awareness dissolves suffering.

Gabor Maté—"The Wisdom of Anger"
A perspective that helped me see anger as a messenger, not an enemy.

Michael Singer—"The Art of Letting Go"
A teaching that softened the way I move through difficult emotions.

Tara Brach—"Radical Compassion"
A practice of meeting yourself and others with presence and truth.

Scott Miller—"Conversations on Self-Awareness and Emotional Responsibility"
Scott's honest, humble approach to leadership helped me understand that emotional intelligence is not a soft skill—it's the core of leadership excellence.

SPIRITUALITY AND WISDOM TRADITIONS

Spirituality has always been a quiet undercurrent in my life—never loud, never forced, never ornamental. It was simply present, like water: carrying me when I needed guidance, grounding me when I felt disconnected, reminding me that leadership is ultimately an act of service.

These texts and teachers deepened my understanding of presence, purpose, forgiveness, compassion, and the unseen forces that shape the human heart. They helped me answer questions I didn't yet know how to ask. They taught me to trust life, to listen inwardly, and to see the divine in everyday interactions—with guests, with teams, with family, with strangers.

This collection is not about religion.
It's about meaning.
It's about returning to what is true.
It's about the part of us that knows, beyond thought, that we are connected.

Books That Opened Me to the Spiritual Dimensions of Leadership and Life

The Seven Spiritual Laws of Success — Deepak Chopra
A simple, elegant guide that taught me to redefine success as alignment, not achievement. Chopra helped me understand that leadership begins in the invisible world — in intention, energy, and coherence.

A Return to Love — Marianne Williamson
A book that opened my heart and reintroduced me to the idea that love is not an emotion — it is a way of seeing. It helped me soften, forgive, and lead with generosity.

A Course in Miracles — Helen Schucman
A lifelong study in perception. ACIM taught me that fear and love are the only two states of mind — and that forgiveness is the bridge back to reality.

The Alchemist — Paulo Coelho
A reminder that our journey is a return to ourselves. This book helped me trust that the universe meets you with guidance when you move with courage.

The Kybalion — Three Initiates
A foundational text that shaped my understanding of consciousness, vibration, polarity, and mentalism. It helped me see life through the lens of universal law.

The Impersonal Life — Joseph Benner
A quiet, humbling text that invited me to dissolve ego and listen to a deeper intelligence within.

The Power of Awareness — Neville Goddard
Neville taught me that imagination is not escapism — it is creation. His work helped me understand intention at a spiritual level.

The Four Agreements — Don Miguel Ruiz
Simple truths with deep spiritual roots. They became anchors in my personal evolution: be impeccable with your word, don't take things personally, avoid assumptions, always do your best.

The Mastery of Love — Don Miguel Ruiz
A beautiful exploration of self-love, forgiveness, and emotional clarity.

The Book of Awakening—Mark Nepo
A daily invitation to see life through the lens of the heart—tender, poetic, wise.

Be Here Now—Ram Dass
A guide to presence that blends spirituality and humanity with beautiful simplicity.

The Prophet—Kahlil Gibran
Poetry that reveals universal truths—about love, work, children, joy, sorrow, and the human condition.

Sacred Texts That Shaped My Inner World

The Bible (Proverbs, Psalms, John)
Timeless lessons on humility, compassion, forgiveness, and the responsibility to serve with kindness. These passages shaped my earliest understanding of leadership as stewardship.

The Bhagavad Gita
A profound dialogue on duty, surrender, and the battle within. This text taught me to align my actions with purpose, not attachment.

The Tao Te Ching—Lao Tzu
A work of deep wisdom. It taught me that leadership is rooted in flow, humility, and effortless intention.

The Dhammapada
Poetic teachings on discipline, awareness, and compassion that have stayed with me for years.

Books on Consciousness, Divinity, and Universal Law

The Untethered Soul—**Michael A. Singer**
A spiritual manual for letting go. It helped me understand that openness is the gateway to peace.

The Surrender Experiment—**Michael A. Singer**
Singer's life became a testament to what happens when we trust the flow of life.

Conversations with God—**Neale Donald Walsch**
A reminder that we are always in dialogue with the universe—through intuition, synchronicity, and truth.

The Hidden Messages in Water—**Masaru Emoto**
A poetic scientific exploration of vibration and intention.

The Law of One—**the Ra Material**
A deeper exploration of unity consciousness.

Podcasts and Conversations That Deepened My Spiritual Inquiry

Know Thyself Podcast—**"Awakening to Your True Identity" with Rupert Spira**
A quiet, profound dialogue on the nature of awareness and the illusion of separation.

Know Thyself Podcast—**"The Nature of Consciousness" with Michael Beckwith**
A powerful conversation about purpose, service, and spiritual alignment.

Know Thyself Podcast—**"The Journey of the Soul" with Ram Dass**
A beautiful exploration of death, love, and the freedom found in surrender.

Oprah's Super Soul Conversations—**Various Episodes**
Oprah's ability to bring spirituality into everyday life expanded my understanding of compassion and grace.

The Higher Self With Danny Morel—**"Oneness and the Return to the Self"**
A conversation that helped me trust the intelligence of surrender and the truth of oneness.

On Purpose with Jay Shetty—"Stillness, Ego and Peace"
A grounded, gentle exploration of spiritual presence in modern life.

Films and Documentaries That Deepened My Connection to the Invisible

Awake: The Life of Yogananda
A portrait of devotion, presence, meditation, and the path of awakening.

Ram Dass: Going Home
A tender exploration of life, aging, dying, and the freedom found in surrender.

Fantastic Fungi
Not a spiritual film on the surface—yet deeply spiritual in its message about interconnectedness.

Inner Worlds, Outer Worlds
A documentary that explores consciousness, frequency, and the sacred geometry of existence.

Talks, Speeches, and Teachers Who Changed My Thinking

Wayne Dyer—"The Power of Intention"
A talk that helped me understand manifestation not as magic but as alignment.

Deepak Chopra—"The Nature of Reality"
A profound exploration of consciousness and the mechanics of the universe.

Neville Goddard—"Imagination Creates Reality"
Recordings filled with timeless wisdom on consciousness and creation.

Byron Katie—"The Work"
A process that taught me to question my thoughts as a path to inner freedom.

Roshi Joan Halifax—"Edge States"
A powerful talk on compassion, suffering, and the emotional thresholds of leadership.

Michael Beckwith—"Visioning: The Empowered Path"
A spiritual framework for aligning with your highest self.

FICTION THAT EXPANDS THE SOUL

Long before I learned leadership frameworks, before I understood presence or consciousness, fiction taught me what it means to be human. Novels became mirrors, revealing the beauty and complexity of the human condition: love and loss, belonging and loneliness, triumph and heartbreak, forgiveness, dignity, courage, cruelty, compassion.

Fiction helped me see people more fully.
It taught me to look beyond behavior and into story.
It softened me.
It grounded me.
It expanded my empathy in ways no textbook could.

These books live at the intersection of imagination and truth—stories that opened my heart, shaped my worldview, and helped me understand humanity more deeply.

Novels That Opened My Heart and Deepened My Empathy

The Kite Runner—Khaled Hosseini
A story of friendship, betrayal, guilt, and redemption. This book taught me that forgiveness can be the most courageous act a human being can undertake.

A Thousand Splendid Suns—Khaled Hosseini
A heartbreaking novel about resilience, sacrifice, and the strength of women. It expanded my understanding of suffering, dignity, and love.

To Kill a Mockingbird—Harper Lee
A timeless reminder that empathy begins with learning to see the world through someone else's eyes. This story shaped my sense of justice and compassion.

The Little Prince—Antoine de Saint-Exupéry
A simple story that carries the deepest truths. It taught me that what matters most cannot be seen—it must be felt.

The Alchemist—Paulo Coelho
A novel that revealed the spiritual journey beneath every human journey. It reminded me that destiny always leaves a trail for us to follow.

Siddhartha—Hermann Hesse
A poetic exploration of awakening, identity, and the soul's evolution. This book taught me that wisdom must be lived, not learned.

The Great Gatsby—F. Scott Fitzgerald
A story that reveals the emptiness of chasing validation and the illusion of the dream. It taught me about longing, illusion, and the human need to feel enough.

The Old Man and the Sea—Ernest Hemingway
A profound meditation on endurance, dignity, and the quiet courage it takes to keep going.

The Book Thief—Markus Zusak
A beautiful reminder of love, humanity, and connection in the midst of darkness.

The Catcher in the Rye—J.D. Salinger
A story about adolescence, vulnerability, and the parts of ourselves we hide to survive.

The Road—Cormac McCarthy
A stark, beautiful story of love, survival, and the fierce tenderness between a father and son.

Stories That Taught Me About Leadership, Identity, and Humanity

The Shadow of the Wind—Carlos Ruiz Zafón
A novel about memory, identity, and the stories that shape our lives. It reminded me that every person carries hidden chapters.

Shantaram—Gregory David Roberts
A sprawling story about redemption, belonging, and the complexity of good and evil.

The Count of Monte Cristo—Alexandre Dumas
A tale of justice, betrayal, revenge, and ultimately forgiveness. It taught me that transformation is more powerful than triumph.

Life of Pi—Yann Martel
A story about survival, spirituality, and the narratives we create to make sense of life.

The Nightingale — **Kristin Hannah**
A powerful novel about courage, love, sacrifice, and the resilience of the human spirit.

The Giver — **Lois Lowry**
A reminder that a world without emotion, risk, or pain is not living — and that true freedom lies in choice.

Modern Fiction That Continues to Shape My Inner World

A Man Called Ove — **Fredrik Backman**
A story of grief, loneliness, and unexpected connection. It taught me that we often have no idea what silent battles people are fighting.

Klara and the Sun — **Kazuo Ishiguro**
A quiet, beautiful exploration of consciousness, care, and what it means to love.

The Midnight Library — **Matt Haig**
A meditation on regret, possibility, and the infinite versions of ourselves.

The Light We Lost — **Jill Santopolo**
A story about love, timing, and the choices that shape our lives.

Anxious People — **Fredrik Backman**
A reminder that human beings are complex, contradictory, and trying their best — even when it doesn't look that way.

Short Stories and Myths That Shaped My Humanity

The Metamorphosis — **Franz Kafka**
A metaphorical exploration of identity, alienation, and the longing to be understood.

The Boy, the Mole, the Fox and the Horse — **Charlie Mackesy**
A tender book about kindness, courage, and vulnerability.

The Hero's Journey — **Joseph Campbell**
Not fiction in the traditional sense, but the framework behind every great story — and every great transformation.

Films and Storytelling That Expanded My Empathy

The Pursuit of Happyness
A reminder that perseverance and love can overcome unimaginable hardship.

Life is Beautiful
A story that reveals the courage of protecting innocence in the midst of darkness.

Coco
A celebration of memory, family, ancestry, and identity.

The Green Mile
A story about compassion, justice, and the unseen spiritual world.

The Shawshank Redemption
A powerful meditation on hope, resilience, and dignity.

The Secret Life of Walter Mitty
A reminder of the beauty in stepping beyond fear and embracing life fully.

PODCASTS, EPISODES, AND TRANSFORMATIVE CONVERSATIONS

Some of the greatest teachers of my adult life did not come to me through books—they came through conversations. Voices that challenged my assumptions, expanded my worldview, softened my heart, deepened my consciousness, and sharpened my leadership.

Podcasts became a form of modern mentorship—a way to sit at the table with some of the most brilliant minds of our time, to learn from their stories, their failures, their disciplines, and their humanity.

These episodes arrived exactly when I needed them: during long flights, early morning walks, meditations, drives, or quiet moments at home. They acted as companions on my journey—reminding me that growth comes in every form and that wisdom is always speaking, if we choose to listen.

Below is a curated list of the episodes and voices that shaped my evolution as a leader, father, husband, teacher, and human being.

The Know Thyself Podcast

Few platforms have influenced me as deeply as *Know Thyself*. André Duqum's conversations bridge ancient wisdom, modern science, emotional healing, and spiritual awakening with mastery, humility, and presence. His ability to create a safe space for truth has made this one of the most important sources of growth in my life.

Here are the episodes that shifted me:

"Healing the Nervous System" with Irene Lyon
A profound exploration of trauma, regulation, and the body's innate intelligence. It helped me understand emotional safety as the foundation for leadership.

"Transcending the Mind" with Dr. Joe Dispenza
One of the clearest explanations of consciousness I've ever heard. It deepened my understanding of coherence, meditation, and the biology of change.

"Remembering Who You Are" with Gabor Maté
A powerful dialogue about suffering, compassion, and the illusions that keep us trapped.

"Awakening the Body's Intelligence" with Thomas Hübl
A masterclass in collective trauma, presence, and energetic attunement.

"The Power of Presence" with Eckhart Tolle
A reminder that awakening is a daily practice.

"The Nature of Consciousness" with Rupert Spira
A quiet, profound conversation about awareness itself. It reconnected me to the simplicity of being.

The Higher Self With Danny Morel

Danny's voice has been a companion in my spiritual journey—honest, direct, unfiltered, and rooted in truth.

"Your True Essence"
A conversation that reminded me that identity is not who we have become—but who we have always been beneath the layers.

"Healing the Inner Child"
A powerful exploration of emotional wounds, parenting, conditioning, and the courage required to break generational patterns.

"Awakening, Oneness and Returning to Source"
A conversation that helped me deepen my faith in surrender, trust, and the intelligence of consciousness.

Huberman Lab

Andrew Huberman is unmatched in his ability to translate complex science into practical tools.

Here are the episodes that shaped my understanding of energy, focus, emotion, and consciousness:

"How to Improve Focus and Resist Distraction"
This episode helped me refine my relationship with attention and presence—both personally and professionally.

"The Science of Emotions and Stress"
A transformative explanation of how the nervous system works.

"Using Vision, Breath and Movement to Regulate Your State"
A masterclass in energy management.

On Purpose with Jay Shetty

Jay Shetty brings spirituality into everyday life with simplicity and heart.

"Stillness, Ego and True Purpose"
An accessible and profound exploration of spiritual principles.

"Letting Go of What No Longer Serves You"
A beautiful guide to emotional release and inner clarity.

"Relationships, Attachment and Conscious Love"
A conversation that helped me grow as a husband and father.

Tim Ferriss Show

"Jim Collins: The Return"
One of the best leadership interviews ever recorded—humility, discipline, and purpose at their highest expression.

"Jack Kornfield: The Art of Letting Go"
A deep dive into presence, compassion, and healing.

"Rick Rubin: Creativity, Awareness and the Inner Voice"
A stunning reminder that creativity is consciousness in motion.

The Rich Roll Podcast

"Steven Kotler—The Science of Flow"
A brilliant exploration of peak performance and human potential.

"Gabor Maté—The Cost of Emotional Repression"
A conversation that tied together trauma, compassion, and truth.

"Mirna Valerio—Courage, Identity and the Human Spirit"
A story that expands empathy and resilience.

Oprah Supersoul Sunday

"Eckhart Tolle—The Deepest Truths of Presence"
A landmark conversation that helped millions awaken.

"Iyanla Vanzant—Truth-Telling and Emotional Freedom"
A gentle, powerful reminder of accountability and grace.

"Caroline Myss—Sacred Contracts and Purpose"
A conversation that opened my understanding of intuition and spiritual identity.

FILMS, DOCUMENTARIES, AND STORYTELLING THAT MOVE US

There are some truths that can't be taught by books or lectures. Some truths must be *felt*. They must enter through the heart, bypass the intellect, and leave us changed—softer, wiser, more awake.

Film does this in a way nothing else can.

The right story, at the right moment in your life, can become a teacher, a mirror, a disruption, or a revelation. These films and documentaries shaped my empathy, expanded my emotional range, challenged my worldview, and deepened my understanding of humanity.

In hospitality—and in leadership—this matters. Because every person you meet is carrying a story you cannot see. Films help you remember that.

Here is the cinema that shaped my consciousness.

Films That Deepened My Humanity

The Pursuit of Happyness
A story of relentless hope and the quiet courage of a father's love. It taught me the dignity found in perseverance.

Life is Beautiful
A film that showed me that compassion can be a form of resistance—and that love can transform even the darkest circumstances.

The Shawshank Redemption
A powerful meditation on hope, inner freedom, and the resilience of the human spirit.

The Green Mile
A story that reveals the unseen emotional and spiritual worlds within people. It taught me to look deeper.

Forrest Gump
A reminder that innocence, presence, and kindness are superpowers in a world that often prizes complexity.

The Secret Life of Walter Mitty
A film that awakens the desire for adventure, creativity, and a life lived fully.

The Boy Who Harnessed the Wind
A story of vision, innovation, and the courage to believe in possibility.

Films on Purpose, Identity, and Emotional Truth

Good Will Hunting
A powerful look at trauma, potential, and the healing that happens when someone finally sees you.

Dead Poets Society
A reminder that leadership can awaken the human spirit—and that courage begins with one brave voice.

A Beautiful Mind
A moving exploration of genius, mental health, and the meaning of love.

The King's Speech
A story about fear, vulnerability, and the courage to lead from authenticity.

The Intouchables
A beautiful story about unlikely friendship and the power of connection.

Modern Films That Inspire Conscious Living

Soul
A film about purpose, presence, passion, and what it really means to live.

Coco
A celebration of ancestry, identity, and remembering where you come from—something deeply aligned with your story.

Arrival
A profound meditation on time, communication, and the emotional cost of knowing the future.

Her
A quiet look at loneliness, connection, and the evolution of consciousness.

Inside Out
A beautiful exploration of emotional complexity that has taught millions how to understand themselves.

Documentaries That Shifted My Perception

Heal
A powerful documentary on the mind-body connection, emotional healing, and the science of transformation.

The Wisdom of Trauma — Gabor Maté
A film that reframed my understanding of suffering and compassion.

Stutz
A vulnerable portrait of therapy, creativity, grief, and personal truth.

Fantastic Fungi
A breathtaking documentary on consciousness, nature, interconnectedness, and healing.

InnSaei — The Power of Intuition
A film that explores emotional intelligence, presence, and the intelligence beneath thought.

Jiro Dreams of Sushi
A masterclass in craftsmanship, excellence, and devotion to one's art — deeply tied to hospitality and mastery.

Minimalism
A reminder that simplicity creates space for presence.

Documentaries on Leadership, Humanity, and Purpose

The Last Dance
A powerful look at leadership, ego, team dynamics, and the cost of greatness.

Chef's Table
A series that celebrates mastery, creativity, discipline, and the emotional story behind excellence.

The Playbook
Coaches revealing the philosophies behind winning, resilience, and team culture.

Won't You Be My Neighbor? (Mr. Rogers documentary)
A tender portrait of kindness as leadership — one of the most moving documentaries I've seen.

Films That Expand Consciousness and Spiritual Awareness

Awake: The Life of Yogananda
A spiritual portrait that inspired me to deepen my meditation practice.

Ram Dass: Going Home
A film that softened my understanding of surrender, aging, and death.

Inner Worlds, Outer Worlds
A documentary that explores consciousness, frequency, and the unseen structures that shape reality.

The Shift—Wayne Dyer
A story that echoes the journey from ambition to meaning—a shift I experienced personally.

Teachers of Consciousness and Inner Freedom

Eckhart Tolle—"The Depth of Stillness"
A reminder that presence is not a technique; it is the natural state beneath the mind's noise. This talk brought me back to the essence of being.

Michael A. Singer—"The Art of Letting Go"
A life-changing transmission on surrender, openness, and emotional freedom. This teaching helped me soften my resistance to life.

Rupert Spira—"The Nature of Awareness"
A beautifully clear explanation of non-duality and the true self. Spira's presence taught me as much as his words.

Ram Dass—"Be Here Now"
A talk that blends spirituality and humanity with humility and humor—a timeless invitation to presence and compassion.

Teachers of Healing, Wholeness, and Compassion

Gabor Maté—"The Wisdom of Trauma"
A talk that changed my understanding of suffering. Maté helped me see pain as a story that needs compassion, not judgment.

Tara Brach—"Radical Compassion"
A gentle, profound teaching on forgiveness, acceptance, and meeting yourself with honesty.

Byron Katie—"Loving What Is"
A reminder that freedom begins with questioning our own thoughts.

Dr. Nicole LePera—"Healing the Inner Child"
A modern teaching on nervous system awareness and emotional healing.

Teachers of Purpose, Vision, and Spiritual Leadership

Wayne Dyer—"The Power of Intention"
A talk that helped me understand manifestation as alignment with one's true nature.

Deepak Chopra—"The Future of Wellbeing"
A synthesis of science, spirituality, and the path to higher consciousness.

Michael Beckwith—"Visioning: The Empowered Path"
A powerful teaching on awakening, purpose, and surrendering to a higher calling.

Neville Goddard—"Imagination Creates Reality"
A timeless reminder that our inner world shapes the outer one.

Sadhguru—"Inner Engineering: A Technology for Wellbeing"
A modern perspective on ancient practices that deepen awareness and peace.

Teachers of Leadership, Service, and Human Excellence

Simon Sinek — "How Great Leaders Inspire Action" (TED)
A talk that reshaped modern leadership. Purpose before power.

Brené Brown — "The Power of Vulnerability" (TED)
A cultural shift in leadership — showing vulnerability as courage, not weakness.

Admiral William McRaven — "Make Your Bed"
A profound reminder of discipline, humility, perseverance, and the importance of small acts.

Patrick Lencioni — "The Truth About Teamwork"
A teaching on trust, conflict, clarity, and responsibility — the foundation of healthy teams.

Scott Miller — "The Messes That Make Us Better"
Scott's honesty and humility taught me that leadership is an act of growth — not performance.

Stephen R. Covey — "Principle-Centered Leadership"
A masterclass in integrity, character, and emotional responsibility.

Teachers of Human Potential, Energy, and Transformation

Dr. Joe Dispenza — "The Formula for Change"
A scientific explanation of how intention, focus, and coherence shape our lives. This teaching grounded my understanding of human potential.

Gregg Braden — "The Science of Compassion and Coherence"
A fusion of science and spirituality that changed my understanding of the heart's intelligence.

Sadhguru — "The Mechanics of the Mind"
A clear, practical look at consciousness through the lens of ancient wisdom.

Marianne Williamson — "The Power of Forgiveness"
A profound talk that taught me forgiveness is emotional liberation.

Teachers of Creativity, Meaning, and the Human Spirit

Rick Rubin—"Creativity and Surrender"
A reminder that creativity comes from stillness—not effort.

Ken Robinson—"Do Schools Kill Creativity?" (TED)
A beautiful perspective on human potential, creativity, and the environments that allow people to flourish.

Elizabeth Gilbert—"Your Elusive Creative Genius" (TED)
A talk about creative identity, fear, and the permission to express oneself.

Work Cited

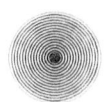

Chapter 1

- Jorgenson, Eric (Ed.). *The Almanack of Naval Ravikant: A Guide to Wealth and Happiness*. Magrathea Publishing, 2020.

Chapter 2

- Frankl, Viktor E. *Man's Search for Meaning*. Beacon Press, 2006.
- Hawkins, David R. *Power vs. Force: The Hidden Determinants of Human Behavior*. Hay House, 1995.
- Hawkins, David R. *The Map of Consciousness Explained: A Proven Energy Scale to Actualize Your Ultimate Potential*. Hay House, 2020.
- Dispenza, Joe. *Breaking the Habit of Being Yourself: How to Lose Your Mind and Create a New One*. Hay House, 2012.
- Dispenza, Joe. *You Are the Placebo: Making Your Mind Matter*. Hay House, 2014.

Chapter 3

- Jung, C. G. "Aion: Researches into the Phenomenology of the Self." In *Collected Works of C.G. Jung*, Vol. 9, Part 2. Princeton University Press, 1978.

Chapter 4

- Jung, C. G. *Modern Man in Search of a Soul*. Routledge, 2001. (Original work published 1933.)

Chapter 5

- Thich Nhat Hanh. *The Art of Communicating*. HarperOne, 2013.
- Dyer, Wayne W. *The Power of Intention: Learning to Co-create Your World Your Way*. Hay House, 2004.

- Childre, Doc, and Howard Martin. *The HeartMath Solution: The Institute of HeartMath's Program for Engaging the Power of the Heart's Intelligence*. HarperOne, 1999.
- McCraty, Rollin, Atkinson, M., Tomasino, D., and Bradley, R. "The Coherent Heart: Heart–Brain Interactions, Psychophysiological Coherence, and the Emergence of System-Wide Order." *Integral Review* 5, no. 2 (2009): 10–115.
- Clear, James. *Atomic Habits*. Avery, 2018.

Chapter 6 *(no new named citations beyond existing references)*

- Van der Kolk, Bessel. *The Body Keeps the Score*. Viking, 2014.
- Maté, Gabor. *When the Body Says No*. Wiley, 2003.

Chapter 7

- Hawkins, David R. *Power vs. Force*. Hay House, 1995.
- Dyer, Wayne W. *The Power of Intention*. Hay House, 2004.

Chapter 8

- Adler, Alfred. Quote widely attributed; consistent with themes in *The Individual Psychology* of Alfred Adler.
- Hatfield, Elaine, John T. Cacioppo, and Richard L. Rapson. *Emotional Contagion*. Cambridge University Press, 1994.
- Rizzolatti, Giacomo, and Craighero, Laila. "The Mirror-Neuron System." *Annual Review of Neuroscience* 27 (2004): 169–192.
- Maté, Gabor. *When the Body Says No*. Wiley, 2003.

Chapter 9

- Hawkins, David R. *The Map of Consciousness Explained*. Hay House, 2020.

Chapter 10

- Drucker, Peter F. *Management: Tasks, Responsibilities, Practices*. Harper & Row, 1974.
- Porges, Stephen W. *The Polyvagal Theory: Neurophysiological Foundations of Emotions, Attachment, Communication, and Self-Regulation*. W.W. Norton, 2011.
- Hatfield, Elaine, John T. Cacioppo, and Richard L. Rapson. *Emotional Contagion*. Cambridge University Press, 1994.

- Rizzolatti, Giacomo and Craighero, Laila. "The Mirror-Neuron System." *Annual Review of Neuroscience* 27 (2004): 169–192.
- Hawkins, David R. *Power vs. Force*. Hay House, 1995.

Chapter 11

- Lair, Jess. *I Ain't Much, Baby—But I'm All I've Got*. Harper & Row, 1976.
- Tsabary, Shefali. *The Conscious Parent*. Hodder & Stoughton, 2010.
- Perel, Esther. *Mating in Captivity*. Harper, 2006.
- Kennedy, Becky. *Good Inside*. Harper, 2022.

Chapter 12

- Gandhi, Mahatma. Quote widely attributed; consistent with themes in *The Collected Works of Mahatma Gandhi*.

Chapter 13

- Aristotle. Quote traditionally attributed; reflective of themes in *Nicomachean Ethics*.
- Porges, Stephen W. *The Polyvagal Theory*. W.W. Norton, 2011.
- Lipton, Bruce H. *The Biology of Belief*. Hay House, 2005.
- Goleman, Daniel. *Emotional Intelligence*. Bantam Books, 1995.
- Clear, James. *Atomic Habits*. Avery, 2018.
- van der Kolk, Bessel. *The Body Keeps the Score*. Viking, 2014.
- Maté, Gabor. *When the Body Says No*. Wiley, 2003.

About the Author

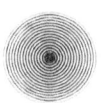

David Arraya is a global hospitality executive, leadership mentor, keynote speaker, and the founder and president of Conscious Hospitality Unlimited—a human development studio and consultancy dedicated to elevating leadership through presence, authenticity, intention, and empathy.

With more than two decades of experience across the world, David has led some of the most renowned luxury hotels and wellness destinations, including Six Senses Ibiza, Four Seasons Hotels and Resorts in Lanai and Austin, Auberge Resorts in Aspen and Riviera Maya, EAST Hong Kong, Fontainebleau Miami Beach, and The Pierre in New York. His leadership journey has taken him across eleven countries and taught him that the soul of hospitality lies not in service, but in consciousness.

He currently serves as the general manager of SHA Wellness Clinic Spain, one of the world's leading wellbeing destinations, where he brings a human-centered philosophy of conscious leadership into daily operational excellence.

David is also the host of *The Conscious Hospitality Podcast*, where he engages visionary leaders, creators, athletes, and change-makers in conversations about leadership, wellbeing, and the future of human potential.

Born in Bolivia and shaped by a global upbringing, David now lives in Spain with his wife, Jessica, and their three children—Andrés, Cruz, and Luna—who remain at the heart of his leadership philosophy.

BOOK DAVID ARRAYA
TO SPEAK WITH YOUR TEAM, PROGRAM, OR ORGANIZATION

David Array is also a sought-after keynote speaker, sharing his vision of conscious leadership and hospitality with audiences around the world. He has spoken for organizations such as **American Express**, **Siemens Healthcare**, **Les Roches**, and **Relais & Châteaux**, inspiring leaders to elevate performance, deepen human connection, and unlock their fullest potential.

To book David for your next conference, leadership retreat, or company event, please contact his speaking agents at the Gray & Miller at **graymilleragency.com**

Representing a community of authors whose books have collectively sold hundreds of millions of copies, the founders of The Gray + Miller Agency launched Maison Vero, a professional publishing house that partners with rising authors to bring their thought leadership to the world. Our representation covers every aspect of thought leadership, including U.S. senators, governors, and ambassadors, billionaire founders and entrepreneurs, researchers, academics, scientists, consultants, practitioners, social influencers, C-suite leaders, adventurers, professional athletes, artists, and creators. We partner with thought leaders and world changers like you who have a story to tell. By bringing decades of professional expertise to our clients, we are charting a new path in a timeless industry that transcends publishing norms, transforming powerful thoughts into impactful books that inspire minds, ignite hearts, and open doors.

Visit maisonvero.com to view our growing list of authors, or to submit a proposal for publication consideration.

Follow Maison Vero for insight and inspiration on social media:

 MaisonVero  MaisonVero  MaisonVeroPublishing

For information about special discounts for bulk purchases, please call 1-949-333-4872 or email info@graymilleragency.com.

Maison Vero is a partner brand of The Gray + Miller Agency, a speaking, literary, and talent consortium. For more information on the talent represented by The Gray + Miller Agency, or to bring any of our thought leaders to your organization or live event, please visit our website at **graymilleragency.com**.